061

£4 23°

D1325899

THE ARTHUR NEGUS GUIDE TO
ENGLISH CLOCKS

The Arthur Negus Guide to English
CLOCKS

DAVID BARKER

Foreword by Arthur Negus

Consultant Editor: Arthur Negus

Hamlyn
London · New York · Sydney · Toronto

For Clarence Jowett,
in acknowledgement of his
great help to me.

Published by
The Hamlyn Publishing Group Limited
London · New York · Sydney · Toronto
Astronaut House, Hounslow Road,
Feltham, Middlesex, England

© Copyright
David Barker 1980

First edition 1980

ISBN 0 600 33198 9

All rights reserved. No part of this
publication may be reproduced, stored in a
retrieval system, or transmitted, in any form
or by any means, electronic, mechanical,
photocopying, recording or otherwise,
without the permission of The Hamlyn
Publishing Group Limited.

Filmset by Photocomp Ltd, Birmingham
Printed in Italy

Frontispiece: Dial of a revolving-ball
moon clock by Thomas Ogden of Halifax
circa 1740. The movement is shown
in Plate 15.

Contents

Foreword by Arthur Negus 6

Introduction 7

1 Clocks and horological terms 13

2 The clock movement 22

3 Dials and hands 37

4 Clock cases 63

5 Lantern clocks 86

6 Long-case clocks 104

7 Bracket clocks 123

8 Wall clocks 134

9 Mass-produced and novelty clocks 144

10 Some notable clockmakers 152

11 Buying and restoring clocks 168

Index 191

Acknowledgements 192

Foreword by Arthur Negus

As everyone well knows, inflation has affected the cost price of antiques particularly over the last decade and perhaps more particularly over the past three or four years, and clocks for some reason did not 'move' at first with other antiques.

It is not all that long ago when a 30-hour long-case clock with a white painted dial in a plain oak case would realise £15-£20 in auction – then, all of a sudden, the prices of all clocks galloped away to the present level.

There is, of course, a lot more to be said about clocks than simply telling the time and David Barker gives, in this book, a composite study of the development of clocks from the 17th century onwards.

In this book, as with all the others in this reference series which is being published (four books have now been published on Furniture, Porcelain and Pottery, Silver and Clocks) the emphasis is on simplicity. We have tried to write books that ordinary folk can readily understand and David Barker's book on Clocks follows this pattern. Everything has been considered and written about, lantern clocks, long-case clocks, bracket clocks, wall clocks, the movement, the dial and the hands; consequently I have no hesitation in recommending this work to you–once again, as with all the other books, knowledge is to the fore.

Arthur Negus

Introduction

In recent years old English clocks have become very popular. Like other antiques, high-quality examples command a premium price; even modest clocks are in great demand. In effect, the last few years have seen a sudden emergence of clocks as an area of interest to collectors. Where for years they had been regarded as unimportant machines simply for telling the time, today more and more people are learning to appreciate the artistic and industrial skill that went in to making even the most common English clocks; others are trying to document this forgotten chapter of English industrial and trade history; and yet others are turning to clocks as a profitable field of investment and a hedge against inflation. Families who have had a few clocks for generations are discovering that their old clocks may represent a wealth of fascination and of potential value; worn but original clocks are being lovingly restored.

In some ways the sudden fascination for old clocks has allowed scope for unscrupulous dealers to exploit the public. Sometimes too, dealers with little or no knowledge of the subject have helped to create a demand and push up prices. It is not uncommon to find – though without any shady intentions on the part of the dealer – examples of a clock and casework of very poor quality, perhaps wrongly married, shabby or with pieces missing, offered at a high price in a local antique shop. On the other hand the revival in interest in old clocks means that there is far more knowledge available for the would-be collector to study his subject before committing himself to a purchase. Whereas 25 years ago ignorance was rife and very few restorers even knew how to reproduce the materials and the movement of old clocks, today it is far easier to find someone to advise you on what is worth buying, what is overpriced, what needs expensive repairs and what is beyond hope. The intention of the present book is to provide the reader with an introduction to the history of the clockmaking industry in England, to describe the various different types of clock that have been made and can still be found for sale, and to help the reader to understand the intricacies of the movements, to explain the qualities of individual clocks and to appreciate how and why a clock is worth restoring.

The English clockmaking industry was, in its heyday in the 17th and 18th centuries, equal to any in the world; it produced large numbers of high-quality clocks, both for specialist precision purposes and for domestic use. Based on the prosperity of the middle classes in the years preceding the industrial revolution, the industry flourished both in London, where the finest and most expensive examples were made, and also in many country towns, the products of which occasionally equal the quality of the London-made clocks, and are full of fascination and imagination in their own right.

Clockmaking in England goes back as far as the Middle Ages, when timepieces were made for installation in the towers of some of the cathedrals, such as in Salisbury. But the domestic clockmaking industry, with which we are principally concerned here, did not properly emerge until the 17th century. At this time clocks were still rare and expensive treasures, and many exquisite examples were produced. In the mid-17th century there was considerable scientific interest in producing extremely accurate clocks, and many notable scientists contributed to the development of new devices. The most important of these developments, claimed to be the invention of Galileo, was the pendulum escapement, which meant that a much higher degree of accuracy could be attained.

The incorporation of these devices in clocks of extremely high-quality craftsmanship brought about a flowering of English clockmaking around the end of the 17th century and the beginning of the 18th; this period has been known ever since as the Golden Age of English clockmaking. The clocks of this date, especially the long-case clocks and bracket clocks, featured fine and delicate movements with long durations between windings, performing complicated striking and chiming feats and even carried astronomical or automated functions.

The long-case clocks, which became in a sense the epitome of the English industry, developed in style until the mid-18th century, when demand fell off in London. The most fashionable clockmakers turned their attention to portable clocks such as bracket clocks, and in the most elegant households the long-case was demoted from the place of honour it had once held. In the provinces, however, a reverse trend took place, and the long-case was taken up by many country makers to cater for the growing market among the prosperous middle classes, who seem to have had little interest in the bracket clock.

In the 19th century, the specialist clockmakers in London

introduced yet more features for better timekeeping in all forms of clock. The distinctive class and provincial tastes of the previous century continued throughout the Victorian period, although, as the long-case became something of a status symbol in the lower-middle and working-class home, it tended to increase in size and decline in quality as the century wore on. Nevertheless, the 19th century witnessed the decline, and indeed the virtual demise of the English industry: large numbers of mass-produced clocks of inferior quality and low price were imported from Germany and the United States. The English clockmakers, who had always organised their industry on a system of craftsman's workshops and apprenticeships, were unable to compete. Many firms went to the wall and many of the traditional skills were lost as clockmakers were forced to diversify their product in order to stay in business at all.

In the early 20th century, clocks were only rarely considered as important items of workmanship or design until the 1960s, when the present revival of interest began. A few people, even so, saw the importance of the field, and built up fine collections of their own. The early years of the century saw the accumulation of the famous Wetherfield Collection which was described by F. J. Britten in 1907, and much of which was sold after Mr Wetherfield's death in 1928. In the 1920s W. Iden began collecting clocks and watches; most of this collection is now in the British Museum

Generally, though, the early and mid-20th century saw remarkably little interest in old clocks. Now it seems almost unbelievable, and very tantalising, that shortly after World War II it was possible to buy rare and beautiful clocks of the 17th century in London for next to nothing.

Today, the situation has changed. It is no longer possible to buy a good clock – and particularly one by a maker of repute – without paying a high price. This no longer only applies to the work of Tompion, Knibb and their like, whose work is anyway mostly in museums, but even to the work of provincial makers who have been recognised widely as producing top-quality work. However, the would-be collector should not despair. There *are* still bargains to be had; enough to make collecting a real possibility. Care is needed in choosing your clocks, and there are many pitfalls for the unwary and those who do not understand the workings of clocks. But the fact remains that thousands of old clocks still survive, and many of them have intrinsic interest and value. I have often been struck by the idea of collecting the clocks of a particular town or region; preferably a local town which had reasonably good clock-

1 Long-case clock by John Farrer of Pontefract, belonging to the author and from which he learned to tell the time.

makers at several different dates. Over the years – patience is a valuable quality for any collector – it should be possible to come across clocks at bargain prices, and you would end up with a probably unique collection of clocks of that town at a fairly modest outlay. It is still not too late for such an enterprise.

This book is intended for the average collector, and I have therefore concentrated on the sort of clocks you are likely to come across in antique dealers' showrooms and salerooms, rather than on the clocks at the top end of the market. Like so many other type of antique, these have become a form of international currency over the last few years, and are collected for their monetary value, not for their worth. The only consolation in this state of affairs is that we can presumably rest assured that they will be kept safe, and will never again be damaged or altered by the ignorant or the unscrupulous.

Personally, I was first drawn towards clocks by my grandfather's love of his old long-case clock, which was a modest but pleasant eight-day clock made by John Farrer of Pontefract in about 1830. For as long as I can remember it stood in the corner of his front room. My family lived next door and it was from the dial of this clock that I learnt to tell the time. I never saw another clock like this one; none of the neighbours had one and my grandfather considered it very rare. He was of course quite wrong, but it was a mistake that was understandable in the period of extraordinary ignorance about clocks, after World War II. But that his pride was misplaced is not important; my fascination with clocks was born from it, and I have been absorbed by clocks ever since. The clock is still with me and I treasure it as much as ever he did (Plate 1).

My reasons for mentioning this clock are twofold. Firstly it illustrates well how a love of clocks can grow up; I am sure that there are thousands of people who remember a vague interest in clocks from their childhood and who would welcome having this interest rekindled by an introduction to the mechanical mysteries of clock design. For these people I have tried to express my own technical interest in the workings of old clocks and show how satisfactory it is, once the basic principles of clock movement design have been grasped, to see the individual and original qualities of each clock that you come across.

The second point to be made about my grandfather's clock concerns the importance of maintenance. A large number of clocks have been looked after very badly over the years; they may have had no maintenance at all, or they may have suffered from the attentions of an unskilled bodger armed with a soft soldering iron and an oily feather. My grandfather, I regret to say, was one of the second sort. He boasted that the clock had never stopped in sixty years, and this was more or less true; but when I inherited it from him in 1972, I found that it was very worn and it had never been properly cleaned. Dust and oil had formed a grinding paste on the pivots and other moving parts; the gut lines were pieced together with bits of nylon fishing line, and the brass hands had been repaired with ugly lumps of soft solder. This clock is by no means untypical. Many long-case clocks, for instance, are driven by weights that are far too heavy, and suffer stress on that account so that, although they may run well for years, they will eventually become worn out and break down entirely. Very few clocks, even today, enjoy the weekly attention of a clockmaker with his clean rag, clock-oiler and pocket chronometer.

As we become conscious of the need for conservation, and as clocks rise in value, it becomes clear that professional restoration is an essential task, to maintain our old clocks in working order. If the parts are replaced as they become worn, and if the intentions of the original clockmaker are respected, there is no reason why a good-quality clock should not last almost indefinitely. Admittedly many of the tasks required to look after an old clock are beyond the amateur, but it is well worth anyone's time to understand how a clock works, how it is liable to become worn and what needs to be done to restore it to a reasonable state.

I hope therefore that this guide will enable its readers to identify styles and periods; to appreciate the quality of a clock, both in appearance and in its mechanics; to understand how to spend their money on clocks wisely; and perhaps, to find themselves drawn into the fascinating subject of the history of clockmaking. Essentially, though, I hope that this book will help its readers to gain as much pleasure from their clocks as I myself have done, for surely with their unique blend of mathematical accuracy, fine metal-working and beautiful wooden cases, they rank among the finest works of craftsmanship, even among the finest works of art.

Chapter 1

Clocks and horological terms

A clock is fundamentally a device that transfers a potential force, whether contained in a lifted weight or in a wound-up spring, into the regular motions of a hand around a dial at a constant and adjustable rate. The clockwork is simply a gearbox which transfers this force into the correct speed and controls it to ensure that it is not used up at an ever-increasing speed. The works also contain similar movements to drive the striking system of the clock, and any other features that may be fitted, such as a date dial, or a second hand. Anyone interested in collecting or owning antique clocks will need to understand the basic principles involved in how a clock works; and the more knowledge that can be built up in this area, the greater will be your enjoyment of looking at clocks. To this end, I have attempted to explain as simply as possible the elements of a clock in the following paragraphs; and then to cover in more detail the meaning of the (inevitably) many technical terms that will crop up, in the form of a glossary for easy reference. Rather than explain the basic terms several times over, those which are defined elsewhere in the glossary are in *italic type*.

The lifted weight or wound spring (whichever is used to drive the clock) applies power directly to the first wheel of the *train*. For a spring-driven clock a device called a *fusée* is introduced at this stage to ensure that the pull of the spring is even, whether or not the clock is fully wound. The train is simply a gearbox which is made up of a series of *wheels* and *pinions*. Its function is to transmit the power to the *motion work* – another set of wheels which divide the power into two, and pass it to the pipes on which the hour and minute hands are fixed. The train (or trains, since extra trains may be added for strikework and other special features) and the motion work together form the *movement*, which is effectively the entire 'works' of the clock. This movement is fixed between two solid metal *plates* held together by *pillars*; the dial is attached to the front plate of the clock, or to a *false plate*, itself fastened to the movement.

The essential element in a clock's design is the *escapement*, which ensures that the movement works at a regular and even pace, rather than at great speed until fully unwound. The escapement is a device by which a catch oscillates at a regular rate, alternately holding back and releasing the last wheel in the train, which is known as the escape wheel. Many forms of escapement have been contrived to regulate the speed of the clock. The earliest clocks used a simple oscillating *foliot balance* or *balance wheel* system; but these were not capable of fine timekeeping. A revolution in clock design was effected by the introduction of the *pendulum* to the escapement. Since a pendulum swings with an absolutely regular beat, it proved an ideal means of ensuring that the escapement worked smoothly and evenly. All that was required was some form of feedback whereby the movement of the escapement also gave an impulse to keep the pendulum in motion. At first a short *bob-pendulum* was used with a verge escapement, but better results were soon achieved with a *seconds pendulum* (which had the convenient beat of exactly one second), connected with an *anchor* or *recoil* mechanism.

This is the essence of the English clock. There are plainly many complications – the device whereby the spring or weight is wound up; the striking mechanism; the means of regulating the clock or driving special features and so on. These have all been described both in the glossary which follows, and in the relevant chapter where each device has had the greatest impact on a particular type of clock.

Anchor escapement The most popular and widely used *escapement* for domestic clocks, from its introduction in about 1675 until today. So-called because of its shape in the form of inverted anchor flukes, the pallets of which act as an escape wheel placed vertically beneath it. In long-case clocks this escapement was commonly used in association with the *seconds pendulum.*

Arbor The arbors in a movement are shafts, pivoted through the plates, on which wheels are fixed. Arbors may also pivot *lifting-pieces* for strike-work. The shaft on which an *anchor escapement* is mounted is known as the pallet arbor.

Balance wheel An oscillating control in the shape of a simple spoked wheel, used in early domestic clocks. The original balance wheel was mounted outside the top plate of the clock and connected directly to the vertically arranged *pallet*-staff.

Barrel A barrel is used for starting and transmitting power to the train of a clock. If the clock is weight-driven, the barrel is directly connected to the winding *arbor*, making key-winding possible. An eight-day clock barrel revolves with its great wheel once in twelve hours; it may be cut with 16 shallow

Anchor escapement

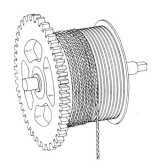

Barrel

grooves. The barrel of an English spring-driven clock has no winding facility; it is simply a round brass box which contains a strong spring. The spring barrel revolves on a fixed arbor and is connected to the *train* by a line which winds from *fusée* to barrel while the clock is running down and the reverse direction when the clock is being wound.

Bell staff The curved steel or iron rod by which the bell is fixed to a striking-clock movement. This is normally fixed to the backplate.

Birdcage Also known as posted movement; used in chamber, lantern and some long-case clocks. It has four vertical posts, one at each corner of the movement, and plates top and bottom.

Blade spring Blade springs give impetus to a hammer in the strike train. They are of a straight shape, diminishing in thickness towards the top to a right angle where they engage with the projection on the hammer *arbor*. They are fixed to the inside of the clock backplate.

Bob pendulum The short pendulum usually associated with the *verge escapement* and lantern clock. It terminates at its lower end in a small pear-shaped brass bob threaded on to its rod.

Boss Name given to a plate or applied tablet on a dial on which the maker's name, a legend, motto or similar may be engraved.

Bridge A bracket having two fixing points, held by screws. This holds the back pivot of an escape arbor at the back of the clock, or, if used in the motion work, it is to support the hour wheels. In the position when it is also supporting the pendulum it is known as a back cock.

Centre seconds Seconds indicated by a large counter-balanced hand radiating from the centre of the dial. Counter-balancing the hand was necessary as the hand was otherwise heavy enough to stop the clock, since it worked directly from the delicately-poised escape wheel. Centre-seconds work is found on long-case clocks, tavern clocks, etc.

Chamber clock The earliest domestic clocks, made from Tudor times until the establishment of the lantern clock in its traditional English form. These clocks were large and of posted-frame construction. They were controlled at first by a *foliot* and then *balance-wheel escapement.*

Chapter ring The detachable ring or circle, on which the chapters or hours are engraved. They are usually made of brass and silvered, but silver chapter-rings are known on some high-quality bracket clocks.

Click So-called because of its actions and the noise it makes; a small piece of steel or iron held loosely by a screw and a spring to retain its tension, and used with a ratchet wheel.

Cock A bracket usually having only one fixing point on the clock plates, used for fixing the reverse minute wheel and occasionally other parts of the motion work including the strike-rack, which is sometimes pivoted. See also *Bridge*.

2 Cock

Collet A collet is a piece of brass driven, brazed or soldered on to an *arbor* and then turned to provide a true running seat with a shoulder on which a *wheel* is mounted. Collets can be plain or decorative and are useful in estimating a clock's age: the older ones are generally large and domed or cheese-shaped behind the shoulder.

Contrate wheel A wheel with teeth on its edge, to transmit the power of the train to the next pinion through 90°, usually to a *crown-wheel* of the *verge* or *balance-wheel escapement*.

Count-wheel The method of regulating strike work used in clocks before about 1675, and sometimes used later for regulating hour-striking and in quarter-chime mechanisms. Sometimes mistakenly referred to as a locking wheel. It is a flat disc with irregular but progressively wider spread slots around its edge. A *lifting-piece* runs along the edge of this wheel during striking, until it reaches a slot, and causes the strike train to be locked up on a separate wheel (the locking wheel). The strike order will only coincide with the time shown on the dial if arranged to do so.

3 Contrate wheel

Crown-wheel The escape wheel of a *verge escapement*, so-called because of its resemblance to a medieval crown, with teeth cut on its edge. The crown-wheel is usually placed at the top of the movement and arranged in a horizontal plane with the points of its teeth uppermost.

Crutch In movements where the pendulum is supported by a flat steel spring from a back-cock, the pendulum is connected to the escapement by the crutch. The crutch is usually riveted into the *pallet arbor* at the arbor's rear end. The connection between the crutch and the pendulum is a sliding fit, sufficient to give impulse to the pendulum and yet keep it as free of the action of the escapement as possible.

Day of the month Date or day of the month indicators are shown on most English clocks. They are worked from an extra wheel or wheels, or a pin arranged in the motion work of the movement.

Dead beat escapement A refined version of the *anchor escapement*. Its *pallets* are shaped to give a positive locking action between beats of the pendulum and no recoil is caused to the escape wheel. The dead beat is more suited to accurate timekeeping than the anchor escapement, and was used on fine regulator types of clock.

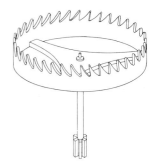

Crown wheel

4 Crutch

5 Fly

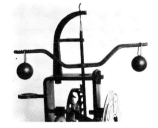

6 Foliot balance

Detent Generally a detent is a part of the movement which detains; such as a lever which drops against a pin to cause the strike to lock up. The term is used for any lever work positioned in a downward plane, particularly if connected with locking or unlocking the strike work.

Dial foot Brass pillar riveted into the dial, by which the dial is pinned to the front plate or false plate. Four dial feet are normal in eight-day long-case work and three in 30-hour clocks. Some later eight-day clocks however use only three.

Dial plate The basic brass plate on which the various rings and decorations of a dial are fixed. Holes for mounting the hands and winding the clock are drilled into the dial plate.

Escapement The escapement imposes measured time upon a clock and keeps it to a regular rate of timekeeping. It usually takes the form of a pair of oscillating *pallets* whose faces intercept the teeth of the escape wheel.

False plate Backing plate to a white or painted dial, fixed close to the dial by four short dial feet, and enables the clockmaker to drill holes and attach to his movements at any convenient place on the false plate's surface.

Finial Ornament forming the topmost terminal of a clock case, made of turned and gilt wood or more usually in brass.

Fly A vane or fan in the shape of a wide flat piece of brass mounted centrally on an *arbor* and arranged to be at the top of the striking train. This regulates the speed of the train by resistance to the air when revolving, giving a measure of rhythm to the strike, when otherwise it would gain speed on a long run such as in striking twelve. It also removes impetus from the strike train and allows smooth locking up on termination of the strike.

Foliot balance A medieval escapement control involving an oscillating bar moving to and fro while attached to a vertical pallet staff working against a *crown wheel*. It could be adjusted by lead weights hung on the foliot arms and moved outwards to slow down the period of oscillation.

Fret Decorative pierced work cut with a fretwork saw or piercing saw in either wood or metal. This may be used on cases, either backed by silk or similar material to let out the sound of the bells, or as decoration only, mounted on a solid wooden ground. This is known as blind fret work.

Fusée A device developed to regulate the uneven pull of a mainspring, which is strong when fully wound and not so strong just before rewinding. The fusée is a cone-shaped drum mounted on the winding *arbor* of the movement and is connected to the *barrel* or drum containing the mainspring by a small chain or length of gut line. Winding the train coils all the line on to the fusée and puts the mainspring in tension. During the running of the clock the spring-barrel revolves and coils the line back around itself. When fully wound the line is pulling on the narrow end of the fusée and therefore requiring a spring's full energy to turn the train.

Gongs The alternative to bells in a striking or chiming clock. These may be either of straight or coiled wire spring. Gongs were not a feature of English work until the 19th century and are never original features on good antique clockwork.

Hood The top part of a long-case clock, which is removable to facilitate access to the movement. Some 17th-century clocks were arranged with a hood, mounted by grooves to the tongued edges of the backboard of the case: they were not removed but slid upwards and held by a catch for access – the so-called rising hood. These hoods had a fixed front with no door. Most clocks however have a hood which has an opening front and which also slide forward for complete removal from the case.

Latch Small flat catch which is pivoted on a screw or loosely riveted to the clock plate, adjacent to a pillar hole. When the plates are put together the latch is turned down to engage in a slot cut in the end of the protruding pillar. Dial feet are sometimes also fastened on in this way.

Leaf Leaves are the teeth of the pinion. A *pinion* proper has fewer than 20 leaves. If it has more then it is technically called a wheel. Usually pinion leaves are of steel.

Lenticle The small circular or oval window in the trunk door of a long-case clock, put in for decorative effect and so that one can see at a glance that the clock is going.

Lifting-piece Lifting-pieces can be found in any part of the movement, but usually in the striking train; they are lifted by a pin to fulfil part of the train's function. Unlocking the strike train is carried out by a lifting-piece situated in front of the reverse minute wheel in the motion work of a movement.

7 Lifting piece

Lunette A lunette on a clock dial is a semi-circular aperture in the lower half of a dial plate centre through which the revolving disc date indicator is viewed.

Maintaining power On most clocks power is removed from the train while winding. In precise regulator clocks, and those with delicate escapements, some form of maintaining power is necessary. One device was Huygens' endless rope principle involving only one weight to drive both going and striking trains. The winding click or ratchet work operating only on the strike side of the clock, causing no interruption in power to the going train when winding.

Moon work The indication of the age and the phases of the moon incorporated into a clock's dial. Four main types of moon work were used: 1) a revolving disc showing the moon's phases pictorially and numerically through a small circular aperture situated just below the XII. Known in London work at the end of the 17th century, it was more frequently used by clockmakers in the area of Halifax, Yorks, in the 18th century and was known as a half-penny or a Halifax moon; 2) a spherical ball moon, divided vertically, half being silvered and half coated with black wax, situated usually in dished portion of an arched dial. This revolves on a vertical shaft, geared from the motion work; 3) the more common moon work in the arch of a clock is a large flat disc with two painted or engraved moons revolving two-monthly. Humps at the sides of the aperture are usually decorated with hemisphere decorations and are supposed to give the correct silhouette to the representation of the waxing and waning moon; 4) on some square dial clocks, white dials and clocks from makers in the north, the moon's aperture is turned upside down and placed in the dial centre underneath the chapter XII.

8 Motion work

Motion work Motion work is the arrangement of wheels and pinions placed on the face of the front movement plate immediately beneath the dial. Their purpose is to transmit the drive to the hands and provide the 12 to 1 reduction necessary for minute and hour indications on the dial. Coupled with this is usually an arrangement for unlocking the strike train.

Movement The total mechanical part of the clock as made by the clockmaker. Horologists refer to this as the movement, others may call it the mechanism or works.

Music barrel A revolving barrel driven from a musical train by a fixed wheel at one end. Pins are arranged in its surface in order to activate the hammers and play the tune on a scale of bells, as the barrel revolves.

Pallets The tips or extremities of an escapement which momentarily stop and check the revolution of an escape wheel. In a *verge escapement* the pallets are sometimes known as flags.

Pillars Pillars may be made in metal or wood and found in a movement or a clock case. They are slender columns and generally shaped like and named after the architectural pillar. Movement pillars of brass hold together the plates of a clock and are found on clocks of both birdcage and plate frame construction. Wooden case pillars are generally seen in the hood, flanking the dial; they may be plain, twisted, or reeded.

Pinion A pinion is a toothed gear which has less than 20 teeth or *leaves*. Often driven by a brass wheel, the pinion leaves are

9 Pinion

formed on the arbors of a movement and the name pinion is sometimes wrongly given to the whole pinion and arbor.

Pivot At either end of an *arbor* is found a reduced portion which forms the pivot on which the arbor revolves through holes in the plates. The pivot is made absolutely parallel and then hardened and polished.

10 Pivot

Plate A sheet of brass used in clockwork. Those most commonly referred to are movement plates between which the wheels and pinions are pivoted to form the movement. The large sheet which forms the basis of a dial is called the dial plate.

Pull repeater A clock which is arranged to repeat the last hour or hours and quarters, on the pulling of a cord. The hours being struck on one bell and the quarters on a smaller one. Thus three blows on the large bell and three on the smaller would indicate quarter to four.

11 Pull repeater

Rack striking The most commonly found strike work on domestic clocks from its introduction about 1675. The action takes place on the front plate of the clock, and the strike is counted by a toothed rack dropping against a cam or *snail*, connected to the hour wheel. The further the drop permitted by the snail the greater the strike. The rack is gathered back to its locked position by a small single toothed pallet and each tooth gathered represents a single blow on the hammer.

Rating nut The threaded nut at the base of the pendulum rod by which the bob may be raised or lowered, thus altering the rate or timekeeping of a clock.

Recoil The recoil is the momentary backward motion made by the escape wheel of an anchor escapement. It is pushed by the action of the pendulum after an escapement pallet has contacted the wheel. At the end of the pendulum's swing in one direction, the wheel exerts pressure on the escapement and gives impulse to the pendulum to maintain its swing.

Repeating work See *Pull repeater*

Seat board The wooden board with appropriate holes and cutaway section, which is fixed in the case to support the clock movement.

Seconds pendulum The pendulum generally associated with a long-cased clock which is 39.14″ and beats one second. It was found to be a convenient size for long-case clocks and its duration meant that the arbor of a 30-toothed escape wheel could be extended forward to provide the drive for a seconds hands.

Signatures The name of the clockmaker and sometimes town or place of business engraved on the dial. Bracket clocks quite often had the name engraved on the decorated backplate also.

12 Snail

Painted dials also carried the maker's name but later in the white-dial period the man whose signature was painted on the dial would most likely be the retailer only.

Silvering The depositing of a silver coating to certain brass parts of a clock dial, prinicpally chapter rings, name-bosses, calendar discs, etc.

Snail A disc cam with twelve levels around its circumference, used in conjunction with a rack whose tail falls against the snail to determine the amount of blows to be struck by the striking train. Since the snail is normally advanced by the hour pipe the number struck always corresponds to the hour shown by the hands. (See *Rack striking*).

Spandrel The spandrel is the triangular space created at the dial plate corners by the rim of the chapter ring. The spandrel may be decorated with engraving, punched decoration or a legend, usually relating to the passage of time. More commonly however a cast brass decoration, loosely known as a spandrel, is applied and held from the back by a single screw.

Throw A hand-cranked lathe on which work is mounted and turned using a hand-held tool.

Train A group of wheels and pinions running in series and with a specified purpose such as telling the time (the going train) or striking the hours (the strike train). These are commonly found side by side in any key wound movement. Another name given to the going train is watch train; W is often found scratched on the winding barrel of an eight-day long-case clock. The strike train maybe referred to as bell train.

Verge escapement An early type of escapement used on domestic clocks. This was developed from the *foliot balance* and *balance wheel escapement*. Both these escapements used a *crown-wheel* in a vertical plane. The verge escapement involved the use of a crown-wheel in the horizontal plan. The pallets on the verge *pallet staff* were controlled by the first *bob-pendulums*.

Weight Usually a lump of lead or iron with a ring or hook at the top to provide motive power for the driving of clock trains. Weights never break down or alter, providing a cheap and constant source of energy, but space is needed in the case or below a wall clock to allow for their descent.

Wheel Brass disc with teeth cut in its periphery, designed to transmit motion, and one of the most basic components of a clock movement.

Winding squares The extended ends of *fusée* or of barrel arbors, shaped to a tapered square section in order to accommodate the winding key, and transmit its circular motion to the spring or lines which are to be wound.

Chapter 2
The clock movement

The clock movement is the most confusing part of a clock for the amateur. It is also, however, the heart of the clock, the part that must be understood to see whether a clock is worth buying, and the area of the clock that most clearly reveals the quality of the whole. It is also, though the novice may not immediately realise this, the part of the clock that was actually made in the workshop of the man whose name appears on the dial, whereas other work, such as the design and construction of the case, may have been put out to a specialist cabinetmaker or a joiner. The clockmaker, his helpers, apprentices and outworkers, on the other hand, will certainly have been responsible for the design of the movement, and for making it up from scratch.

Most successful English clocks were made in metal (although a few have been known in wood), and any study of the history of the clock movement must involve a discussion of the metals used and the engineering principles involved. Although this discussion may seem forbidding at first sight, it is an essential background to any understanding of the qualities of a clock, and the issues at stake in restoring it. In this chapter, I have therefore begun with the basic material, the metals used by the clockmakers. Since most old clockmakers' workshops included the actual making up of most if not all the individual parts, the wheels, arbors, pinions and so on, I have next described the methods used in actually producing these pieces. This aspect of the subject is not only of special fascination to many people, who tend to marvel that old clockmakers could produce such precise movements without the advantage of modern methods, but it is also very necessary to appreciate the quality of the clockmaker's art. The third part of this chapter discusses the various ways in which clockmakers have approached the structural problems of making a movement that will hold together, run smoothly and reliably for many years. I hope that the result is to produce an introduction to the clockmakers' craft as seen from the very practical point of view.

The metals primarily used in the construction of old English clocks are brass and steel. Generally speaking, moving parts, such as the pivots of a clock, need to revolve on a dissimilar metal to prevent rapid wear. This principle is found in modern engineering in the steel and bronze bush; in clocks it means that the plates are usually made of brass, and the arbors or shafts which turn on them are of steel. The way in which brass and steel act on one another is a matter of prime importance. In some cases, the harder metal may, strangely at first sight, be worn away by the softer: for instance, a brass wheel turned by a small steel pinion will tend eventually to wear away the leaves of the pinion while leaving the brass unmarked. The reason for this phenomenon is that grit and dirt tends to become embedded in the soft brass and then grinds away at the harder steel. This is accentuated by the quicker motion of the pinion relative to the wheel. From this example it will be seen that the way in which the metals are used in a clock movement is itself a matter of considerable expertise on the part of the clockmaker.

The yellow brass used in the 17th and 18th century was quite unlike the brass that we have today. Its delicate yellow colour is immediately obvious in contrast to repairs or replacements made in new brass, which looks quite orange in comparison. Specialist restorers have castings made in yellow brass of the old recipe to repair old and valuable clocks more convincingly. Judging by its colour and its nature, the old brass contained tin and possibly more zinc than today's brass. One of the earliest things I learned about restoration of old clocks was not to try and heat up a cracked or broken dial plate in old brass; unlike most brass available today, which is normally softened by heat, this old brass was sure to crack and completely de-nature. Possibly this is due to its method of preparation and age changing its properties. When buying brass today, it is possible to obtain a polished and uniformly thick sheet or round bar of the required gauge. This was not so in the old clockmaker's workshop. The molten brass had to be poured in to a flat mould for sheet and when cold was laboriously beaten, scraped and filed in order to obtain a flat sheet for plates, and discs for wheel blanks, dials and so on. Its surface then was irregular, bearing all the marks of its preparation. More solid parts, such as pillars, cocks and lantern clock finials, and pendulum bobs were rough-cast in sand; round parts were then turned up in a hand-cranked lathe using hand-held cutting tools, and flat parts filed to shape. The high standard of tools and materials is something that we expect today, but their preparation and making was a major time-consuming factor in early workshops. Hours must have been spent in keeping a good edge on cutting tools.

Steel is a word used very loosely when talking about old movements, and just as I have qualified the word brass I must also say something about the nature of steel available to the old clockmakers. In fact it would be more honest to describe it as hardened iron. Various methods were used to harden iron for tools used in cutting and for the working parts of the clock. These methods were developed empirically through experience and were by no means dependable. Each man had his own preference. One clockmaker hardened his pinions by cooling them in a bar of soap, another chose to do it in bacon fat, but generally the iron would be heated to a cherry red and then quenched in cold water. Many 17th-century clocks are found to have very soft pinions and if they have been run regularly and are original, these will be very worn indeed today. Plate 17 shows a set of worn pinions that I replaced from a lantern clock made by Edward Norris of London in about 1670.

In order for a metal to become hard through the process of heating and rapid cooling, carbon must be present. Much of the early iron used was low in carbon content and it was discovered, though not by scientific methods, that if iron was put with charcoal or bone in a simple furnace and subjected to intense heat for a few days, a carbonisation of sorts would occur, though leaving a blistered and scaly finish to the shallow, hardened steel surface. The process was tedious, long

13 *Left:* The back of a lantern clock dial plate, showing its variable thickness and other marks of its preparation. Temple Newsam House, Leeds.

14 *Right:* A selection of clockmakers' screwplates, used to fashion the screws used in various parts of the clock.

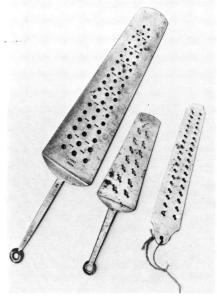

and frequently unsatisfactory in the final analysis.

Crucible steel, the next stage in the development of hardening iron, was unknown in Europe until 1746 when it was developed by the clockmaker, Benjamin Huntsman of Doncaster. Clearly he must have experienced the frustrations just described and, desirous of something better, embarked upon a series of experiments by which he carbonised and made crucible steel by heating small quantities of molten metal in a clay crucible together with wood. The whole was contained in a small conical furnace and blown with bellows for several hours. The improved steel and shorter preparation time was such a success that Huntsman gave up clockmaking, moved to Attercliffe, Sheffield, and became a crucible steel manufacturer on a larger scale.

After discussing the limitations in the materials available and marvelling at the skill of the old clockmaker, we ought to consider how they actually carried out the day-to-day business of clockmaking and what tools were used for what purposes. Round brass parts such as pillars, pipes and small finials were made or bought in as castings and turned up on the throw or clockmaker's lathe. Screws have been made from the earliest times but even at the end of the 18th century tended to be shallow-threaded and highly individual in their form. No deep- or blind-threaded holes were attempted in clockwork and the female threads were usually restricted to the thickness of a clock plate, cock or detent, and these hold surprisingly well. To make a screw, the clockmaker had the use of a screwplate which had a variety of threaded holes cut in it. The screwplate, usually with a small handle at one end, was made by hand-shaping the threaded holes with a hardened male screw matrix. The screws are almost always iron although brass screws, particularly in dial spandrel castings or holding a spring behind a moon dial, are not unknown. Cheese-headed screws and round domed-headed screws are also common and are found on work from every period. Decorative screws are found in high-quality work and in such cases are restricted to features on the backplate which was the area most commonly seen when the case was opened, or in the case of a long-case clock, when the movement was lifted down. These are illustrated in a long-case clock movement of a high quality by Thomas Ogden of Halifax (Plate 15), in which backplate screws resemble the open mouth of a serpent or similar decorative creature.

One of the questions frequently asked about clockwork is how the clockmaker made such accurate and evenly spaced wheels. How did they cut them and how did they decide on the shape of the teeth? We know today that the shapes of the teeth of clock wheels is important, but the old clockmaker did not consider this to be a major problem as it had been overcome successfully by trial and error and the shapes found to be a success were used unchanged in many workshops for decades. A variety of tooth forms are found in old English clocks and early work does not necessarily mean crude work, though early work from a country district frequently was. Crude work might involve flat-topped teeth, irregular depth at the bottoms or roots of the teeth and even leaning teeth, caused by applying the cutter to the blank off-centre. Regular but oddly-shaped tooth forms are also found in later clocks, particularly white-dial 30-hour clocks whose movements were frequently handwrought by country makers well into the 19th century. The well-formed tooth most commonly seen on English work settled into a style resembling an early English or Gothic arch. This shape proved to work very well and was close to the tooth form that we now know to be the ideal shape for clock wheels based on the epicycloid curve. This allows wheels to engage smoothly with their pinions and move freely, provided the correct depth or spacing is observed when laying out the trains.

Dividing the wheels, or providing a means of cutting any

15 *Left:* Movement of a revolving-ball moon-clock by Thomas Ogden of Halifax circa 1740, showing the fine turning and exquisite details in this exceptional clock. Its dial is shown in the frontispiece. Temple Newsam House, Leeds.

16 *Right:* Old Town Clock of York, 1658, formerly in St Williams Chapel, Ouse Bridge. The vertical straps of the frame are held in position by wedges. Museum and Art Gallery, Scunthorpe.

given number of teeth with even spacing, was a little more difficult and in medieval times this probably had to be done by measuring with a tape around the circumference of the wheel blank, then cutting and filing by hand. By the 16th century a mechanical means was devised of mounting a wheel blank rigidly above a plate which had been punched and drilled with a variety of numbers of holes arranged in concentric circles around the diameter; the greater numbers at the rim and the lesser towards the centre. By the end of the 17th century such dividing engines, or wheel cutting engines as they came to be known, were regularly used in the better workshops. These machines served successive generations with little development or alteration, and in common with other valuable machines and tools were passed down from father to son and master to journeyman. With the problem of holding and dividing a wheel solved, another problem yet remained. The cutter, and the method of mounting and revolving it formed the next problem. It was necessary to divide the pitch circle of the wheel blank by the number of teeth required. The pitch circle lies just within the outside diameter of the blank and forms the actual point at which the finished teeth engage with the pinion leaves or teeth of a wheel. Once this division had been made it was halved again to calculate the space to be cut away; the tooth and the space were generally of equal width. At first the teeth cut by the dividing engines were rectangular in shape and square at the tips. The tips were afterwards filed up by hand to the arched shape. Later in the 18th century a special engine called a rounding-up tool was designed to do this separate job. The cutter for the dividing engine was itself shaped and formed from a round piece of hard metal bar, turned or filed to the desired shape and then ground to half its thickness. The tip was then ground back to enable the cutter to cut through brass with the minimum of effort on the hand-cranked machine.

Pinions were difficult to make and their slender shape made them fragile and tricky to hold during the making. At first they were filed up and turned from the solid, being rather more coarse on early chamber and lantern clocks than they were in later clocks. By the late 17th century, however, a method was devised by which pinions were reliably made for over a hundred years. Pinion wire, which was in effect a continuous grooved pinion, was drawn while still hot through a hard draw-plate. Bought from a material dealer or manufacturer, the wire was parted off to the length required. The leafed portion of the pinion was marked round in the throw and unwanted portions removed to form the arbor. More recently pinions have again been worked from a solid round bar, with the leaves cut in specialist machines and the arbor turned smooth in the lathe. This is a more accurate way of forming true leaves since pinion wire was frequently distorted in its manufacture or by the breaking off of the unnecessary leaves along the arbor.

Early clocks had a high proportion of iron in their construction, and medieval, ecclesiastical and similar clocks were almost exclusively made that way, with only occasional brass bushes. Even these may have been the result of later repair, for many iron clocks had pivots driven and then broached into the iron frame in their original construction. Early lantern clocks in iron are not unknown, but by the 17th century it was increasingly unusual to find wheels and plate made in anything but yellow brass. Iron persisted as a material for pillars in some lantern and country long-case clock work. Count-wheels and some cocks were also occasionally made of iron. The items generally made of iron and steel are hammers, locking levers, lifting pieces, and the staff on which the bell sits. These iron parts were filed up from the solid or cast into required shapes pivoted in the lathe where necessary and fabricated by brazing when this was needed. This latter process gave way to silver-soldering, although it is difficult to state when this change occurred.

Unlike engineers and motor mechanics, clockmakers do not secure their clocks together with nuts and bolts, although screws are used for some jobs. These jobs are quite few in number and nothing so ambitious as long blind holes were attempted. In the normal clock of the 17th, 18th and 19th centuries the bell staff is generally secured through the backplate by a steady pin and a single screw. The back cock which provides a pivot or a knife-edge for the escapement arbor as well as the suspension point for the pendulum is also screwed to the backplate in two places. Blade springs and bridges of various types are also held to the plates by screws.

The framework of a clock is usually formed by pillars and plates. It is held together in three main ways; sometimes two of these methods are found on the same clock and they all occurred throughout the period under discussion. Fastening a clock by wedges appears to have been the earliest method used – allowing one bar to pass through a hole in another, cross-drilling the protruding part and fastening the joint with a wedge. This was a blacksmiths' method of fastening together a cage or framework of bars before the era of welding, and it was usual on the earliest clocks, especially iron turret clocks, which can loosely be described as of birdcage construction. The method was strong and had the advantage of being capable of being dismantled again. It was also an easy way in which to build an early iron clock frame and fasten in its upright plates. The smaller chamber clock and the lantern clock continued to use this method of fastening, with subtle variations introduced as the clock became more delicate. Country 30-hour long-case clocks which retained the birdcage layout for their trains also retained the wedge as a means of fastening until as late as the last quarter of the 18th century. When clockmakers started to put the strike and going mechanisms known as trains side by side, the clock plates were placed fore and aft and held together with pillars in a horizontal plane. These were riveted to the backplate; the fronts of the pillars protruded through a hole in the front plate and were cross-pinned by a taper pin pressed into a hole. This method of fastening accounts for 95 per cent of all clocks in period English work. Contemporary with the introduction of this method of fastening, and just as common in later 17th century London work, was the latched pillar in which the protruding end of the pillar was slotted at one side instead of being drilled. The slot was then fastened by a latch or flat hook, which was pivoted by a rivet from the plate. These latches were sometimes decorative and punched with eyes which made them further resemble a bird or a fanciful creature. Latching was the method used almost exclusively by the famous Tompion for all his complicated long-case and bracket clocks and not only for fastening plate pillars, but was also used to attach pillars between dial and front plate.

Occasionally one comes across a clock on which the middle plate pillar, of a five-pillar eight-day movement, is latched, while the four pillars at the corners of the plates are con-ventionally pinned. The explanation for this is that when a clock is being assembled in the clockmaker's workshop it is usual to pin, loosely, two of the pillars, possibly diagonally at top and bottom, before checking all is in order. Also to check that the trains have the correct free movement and that the strike train has the correct relationship of its wheels, hammer pins and lifting pieces and so on to achieve a smooth strike. Once this is found to be in order, the pins can be pressed home firmly. If, as is often the case, the plates have to be parted again momentarily to effect an adjustment, it is much easier to slip aside a single latch in the centre than to push out two pins, which may need the aid of a pair of pliers or other tool.

The method of fastening wheels to their arbors changed

subtly throughout the development of the English clock, and the way in which this was done can help to date the work. If the style is not consistent within a single clock, it can also tell us that there have been repairs or alterations; but more of that in a later chapter. Generally speaking, the stubbier the arbor and collet the earlier the work, though in much early work the collet was not used at all. Early- and mid-17th-century lantern clocks frequently had their wheels squared on to thick arbors. The wheels at this period were thick enough to make this method possible, but accuracy was not guaranteed. Sometimes a shallow seat shape was turned integral with the iron arbor and when drilled the wheel could be mounted direct. This is also found on some early long-case work but it is not common. Brass collets used on lantern clocks and some early case clocks were driven or brazed on to the arbor to form a broad seating for the wheel. This seat was reduced to size and trued after the collet was brazed firm.

The first English clocks took the form of an iron cage with arbors supported by vertical bars; this arrangement was favoured by the maker of smaller domestic chamber clocks and continued into the 17th century in the lantern clock. The fact that in such clocks the strike train was arranged behind the going train was of no importance, as winding was done by pulling on a rope, and clock weights at this time were rarely enclosed so that one had a visual reminder that the clock needed winding every twelve hours or so. However, with the development of the anchor escapement and the seconds pendulum in about 1675, clocks with increased accuracy and a more delicate construction were feasible. Something more delicate than a rope was required to hold the weights of the clocks that were designed to go for increased periods of time. Long lengths of gut needed to be wound on to barrels, turned with a key, and, since the key had to pass through the dial plate, it was necessary to place the going and strike trains side by side. This departure from the medieval birdcage design caused the plates to be arranged vertically and, where they had previously been merely top and bottom plates, they now became integral to the design of the movement, carrying pivots, motion wheels and lever work. Although lantern clocks were still made for many years in London, mainly as travelling alarms, and also in some country regions, most clocks were now made in the new plate form rather than the birdcage form.

The development of ideas was rapid. The golden period of English clockmaking was now begun and clocks were made that would go for periods of one month, three months and even

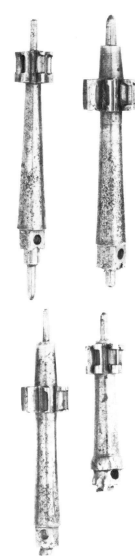

17 Worn-out pinions removed from the lantern clock by Edward Norris, London, shown in Plate 68. It can be seen that the wheels are squared onto these arbors.

a year between windings. Complicated spring-driven bracket clocks were made which would tell the mechanical time and solar time and which struck on great numbers of bells and played tunes. London makers developed horological skills at a rapid rate. Many of the London makers at this time were inventive and capable men, able to work out wheel patterns and the numbering of trains to achieve a specific result. The best craftsmen continued to do so and through the 18th century the work of a good maker was individual and original in execution and concept. As a result dates alone can give a misleading impression of the development of the craft. Contemporary with the fine and sophisticated marquetry-cased London clocks of the 1680s, country styles of clockmaking flourished in the more remote centres, in which the work bears no resemblance to the London clocks. Country clockmakers up to the mid-19th century would probably make only two types of clock: the 30-hour long-case clock and occasionally the eight-day long-case clock for a special order. Bracket clocks, which were driven by springs, had particular problems associated with the type of steel needed for the springs, which was unreliable and difficult to make at this early date. The movements used in country clocks tended to be of a similar pattern and type, probably from a pattern book started by father or master and followed with little inventiveness except perhaps in decoration. It is also likely that country clockmakers would have facilities for cutting only limited tooth numbers on wheels, and so arranged the movements to suit the teeth they could produce.

It is impossible to be dogmatic about the type, shape and materials used for clock weights. More than all other parts, these were lost, sold for scrap, or have been exchanged freely in recent years. Enough clocks remain in their original state, however, to determine some patterns to look for, though this is not always an infallible guide. The earliest chamber clocks had lead weights and counter-weights were used at the reverse end of the rope, particularly in an alarm, to keep it taut. Various shapes from a bell shape to a dumpy pear drop were used, though a parallel weight was often the norm. High-quality hooded wall clocks and the sophisticated long-case clock in the period immediately before and after 1700 used lead weights cased in thin brass. Tops to these weights were carefully turned and screwed on to a threaded bar protruding from the lead. From early to mid-18th century long-case clocks generally had plain uncased lead weights, though high-quality clocks and some precision clocks continued with brass casing until the early 19th century. The white-dial clock period, after 1770, marked the almost universal change from lead to iron for clock weights. Occasionally, especially on later products, the weight of the iron used was lettered and cast at the bottom of the weight. The average weight of a 30-hour long-case weight was 7 lbs, and an eight-day weight 12 lbs. Very occasionally the maker's or ironfounder's name would be cast into the weight also.

The monastery bell was an established way of marking the routine of services and dividing the working day long before clocks were introduced to this country. The Venerable Bede mentions the use of bells in this way at the end of the 7th century. It was natural therefore that a bell should be used to sound the hours on early mechanical clocks. Since nothing better or more pleasing was discovered, this idea was carried over into domestic clock production. Clock bells are almost invariably cast in 'bell metal', a variable alloy composition which usually contained a large part of copper with antimony and tin. It is almost certain that bells were bought in by the clockmaker, not made in his workshop, and bell founding existed as a separate craft from an early period. Travelling bell founders cast church bells on site in the middle ages. This is known to have gone on into the 18th century and since the setting up of clay moulds and pouring the metal was a specialised skill it seems likely that such craftsmen would also make bells for the clockmaker. Bells used in clockwork were never significantly 'bell'-shaped, with rare exceptions, but were instead a flatish domed shape of a circular plan, rather like a deep, inverted saucer. Clocks playing tunes or providing a quarter-chime and so on had a number of bells; often eight bells making a scale, fastened on a bell staff and dished closely inside each other at the top of the movement where they could be struck by the hammers with the smaller bells playing the higher notes. These are referred to in clockwork as a nest of bells. Clock bells can be tuned to achieve the desired note by turning away the metal at various points. From the beginning of the 19th century, spiral wire gongs struck by leather-tipped hammers were used as an alternative on some bracket or table clocks. Sometimes a clock can be found with the tune or quarter-hour chime on bells, and the hours sounded on a gong. These are not generally well regarded and while they were almost always very well made at this period they do not give as pleasing and subtle a sound as an early bell delicately struck by a light hammer. Anything other than a bell in long-case clockwork should be regarded with suspicion. These were

18 *Opposite left:* Anonymous country long-case clock with one hand, dated 1672. Towneley Hall Art Gallery and Museum, Burnley.

19 *Opposite right:* Sophisticated marquetry long-case clock of about 1680, by Matt Crockford, London. Towneley Hall Art Gallery and Museum, Burnley.

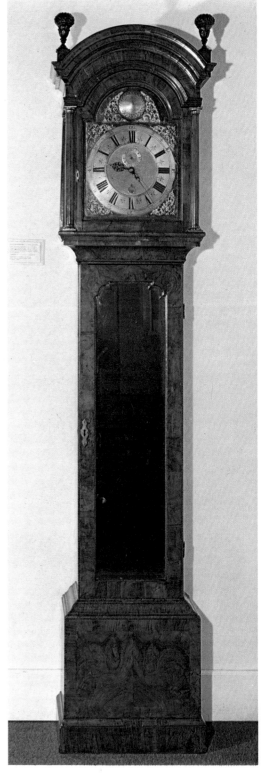

34

20 *Opposite left:* Mulberry long-case clock by Tompion, made in about 1700. British Museum, London.

21 *Opposite right:* Year-clock by William Webster, made in about 1720. A mirror is fitted to the trunk door. British Museum, London.

sometimes altered to arrange the strike on wire gongs screwed into the back of the case and I have even seen a chrome chime tube hanging in the case of an altered clock.

It will be apparent that the skills and methods of making parts of a clock movement are many and various. Few clockmakers possessed all the skills necessary to make a complete clock and even those that did rarely worked alone. Factory methods of splitting up the work into different parts were adopted early on, for we can tell from engravings of early clockmakers' workshops that even chamber clocks were made by division of labour. Thomas Tompion had many helpers at his workshop in Water Lane and from the rate book of 16th July 1695, we see recorded 19 people, two of whom were Tompion and his sister, and the rest were servants, journeymen and apprentices. After buying in of bells and castings such as dial spandrel decorations or finials in rough-cast metal, all the rest would be fashioned and wrought by the men, working long hours under the direction of the master clockmaker. It is often stated that apprentices started their apprenticeship by making clock hands. I have even heard it suggested that they travelled the country taking orders for clocks. There is no factual evidence of this being true, and it would seem to me that both arguments are unlikely. Finely wrought hands are of great importance to a good clock and required skilful sawing and filing up if they were to do justice to a handsome dial. The job of representing the workshop to customers would be done by the master and the important business of discussing a new clock and costing the same would not be entrusted to a mere beginner. Clocks did of course sell on the reputation of a clockmaker and in such cases the orders were dealt with by the master or by a member of the clockmaker's family.

Apprentices would sample all of the skills throughout their seven years of training. Perhaps they would start with base tasks such as preparing brass by hammering and scraping to obtain a surface. They would also make their first observations of the wheel-cutting process by turning the crank to provide power for the cutter. Crossing out wheels (that is, cutting away the unwanted portions in the wheel to provide the crossing or spokes in the wheel centre) would also occupy them. Turning at the lathe, marking out and making of hands would require lots of patience to master the necessary required skills. All of these tasks would have to be learned before specialisation could take place, when obviously a man would have preferences and likely do one job better than another.

Since clock manufacture in the 17th and 18th century was truly laborious and all power was supplied by hand, fitness for purpose was one of the yardsticks in manufacturing, although delicate, decorative touches here and there and beautiful turning have always been a part of English clockmaking. Engraving too has always been used to beautiful effect. The engraved backplate of an English bracket clock is usually a delight to see. Nevertheless the design of the movement of a clock is one of the most important things to those who understand horology. An expert can date a clock and sometimes make an accurate guess at its maker by examination of the movement alone. Within the general framework of craft practices, each maker had his own little way of doing things, whether it be finishing off the head of a screw or engraving a bird's head on the tail of a hammer spring. The good makers had a sense of design and aesthetics which rarely failed them, and it is this along with their mechanical skills which we have come to admire in their work.

22 Engraved backplate of a bracket clock by Henry Jones, London, about 1680.

Chapter 3
Dials and hands

The Man is yet unborn that duly Weighs an Hour

From the dial of an eight day clock
by Thos. Radford of Leeds about 1775

Much as we recognise the character of a person by looking at his face, we are immediately able to gain an impression of a clock by looking at the dial. The quality of the clock is largely reflected in the dial, and if this is of good quality – well-designed, of good proportions and skilfully engraved – then the movement is likely to be so too. At any rate, the legibility and design of the dial is important for obvious reasons and much care was spent, throughout the history of domestic clockmaking, in making them as fine and clear as possible, even though sometimes legibility was sacrificed for the sake of decoration.

Early church clocks, such as the one erected at Salisbury Cathedral in 1386, had no dial at all but struck the passing hours on one of the church bells. This was not unusual in the few public clocks erected and what was not an expected feature in those early days was not missed. The bell recording the hours was quite accurate enough to regulate the ecclesiastical orders and the rural community in the surrounding fields. to people working by sunlight, divisions of less than an hour were hardly relevant at all. The continental idea of using Jacks, carved and jointed figures which struck bells, spread to England in the 16th century and was used on clocks with and without dials. The idea of Jacks in clockwork kept its appeal. Special public clocks incorporating them as a decorative feature have always been built. The modern Jacks clock at Fortnum and Masons in Piccadilly, London, is known throughout the world. Dials of these large public and church clocks, if they existed at all, were made of various materials, sometimes of carved stone if not too large, but mainly of wood. These were built out in an architectural style, not unlike the interior church woodwork decorated with carved mouldings and finials. The whole was finished in bright painted colours and gilt work.

The first domestic clocks in England were scaled-down iron

clocks, and dials were either set to revolve and were marked by a fixed hand in the Continental manner, or were fixed and marked by a revolving hand. This second, later idea has come to be the accepted pattern. Sheet-iron and sheet-brass dials were at first oblong front covers pinned between vertical plates into the front of the clock, the dial markings swept by a single hand for a twelve-hour period being crudely engraved or punched between concentric circles scribed on to this plate. Some early 16th-century spring-driven clocks appear to have had cast brass and gilt cases incorporating their cast and chased dials among the architectural and astronomical pattern work. These were largely of German design, and in many cases executed by Continental craftsmen or their apprentices. By 1600 English characteristics began to appear in clocks whose design had previously been dominated by the Continental influence and craftsmen. It had become usual to make dials with a dial plate and a separate engraved ring with numerals for the hours or chapters (hence the name chapter ring) pinned on to the front. For about 170 years this design became the norm for all dials and later any sub-dials were applied to the dial plate in the same way. Early lantern clocks, which were the first English clocks to be made this way, had a very narrow chapter ring, allowing only about $\frac{3}{4}''$ for the height of the numerals. Its spread was restricted by the distance between the front clock pillars. Since these clocks were not particularly accurate anyway, one hand only was usual. Engraving was therefore simple; Roman numerals with designs such as a crow's foot pattern or a simple star between them, for decorative effect as much as to mark the half-hour. Sometimes only the numbers XII, III, VI and IX were engraved and plus marks sufficed for the other hours. The main decorative area on these very early balance-wheel clocks was within the chapter ring and the engraving continued to be astrological or geometrical, often radial in general arrangement.

By the mid-17th century chapter rings had become slightly wider and covered a greater area of the front of the clock, stretching to outside the width of the clock and a little beyond. Still marked for one hand only, the engraving was more sure and quarter-hour divisions appeared within the ring at the inner edge. The dial centre had now become an engraver's showpiece, with overall foliage and scrolls. Floral bouquets, frequently of tulips or roses, were used. The corners of the dial plate outside the chapter ring were also engraved with simple sprays or leaves to match. Often the clockmaker's name was incorporated in a cartouche at the centre of the dial, usually

23 *Left:* Lantern clock by William Selwood at Ye Mermayd in Lothbury (1635) showing early dial features. A disc for setting the alarm should cover the plain dial centre, but is missing.

24 *Right:* An East Anglian lantern clock with broader chapter ring than its earlier London counterparts. Jeremy Spurgin, the maker, died in 1699.

above the mounting of the hand. No fixed place was used to engrave the maker's name and three places were normal at this time: in a cartouche above the mounting of the hand on the dial plate beneath the chapter ring, or at the base of the front fret which fastened the horizontal top plate of the clock.

Consideration must now be given to the dials of the three main types of clock which became common after the invention and rapid spread of the pendulum. These were the lantern clock, the long-case clock and the bracket clock. Chapter rings on all these types were similar in style though different in size and preparation. Lantern clocks were perhaps a little more crude in some country districts, although very sophisticated lantern clocks do exist with dials and movements made to the highest London standards. The first long-case clocks had square dials with very narrow chapter rings and, because the introduction of the pendulum offered increased accuracy, they had the addition of a minute hand and the resultant marking of the outside edge of the hour circle. It had now become realistic to divide an hour into portions of 60 seconds each and to mark them in the minute circle. Some high-quality clocks towards the end of the 17th century had each minute numerically engraved in full, though this fashion was rare and did not persist. Most dials were engraved in the spandrel corners and the centres could be a riot of beautiful engraving of flowers and foliage. The clockmaker's name was often incorporated among the engraving in the dial centre or even at the base of the dial plate underneath the VI on the chapter ring.

The seconds indicator with its separate ring was not introduced to the dial until after 1672 when the long pendulum beating the seconds became the norm. After this date many features became accepted which remained in the dial's make-up until the demise of the brass-dialed clock. The box calendar with a peep number changing every 24 hours was a feature dating from the last two decades of the 17th century. So too was the matted- or punched-dial centre and the applied cast decorations for the spandrel corners. By 1680 the dial plate of a long-case clock was likely to be 10″ square with a chapter ring of slightly broader proportions than before and simple cast cherub spandrel decorations in the corners, a slim but large seconds ring pinned on to the dial plate in the same way as the chapter ring and engraved with 60 divisions, each five being numbered in Arabic numerals, matt-dial centre and the clockmaker's name at the base of the dial plate. The box calendar was cut in the dial plate just above the VI position. Arabic numerals were commonly used on the calendar engraving. Roman numerals were used for marking the hours on the chapter rings of almost all clocks, and a little error has traditionally been accepted in the numbering for the sake of balance in design of the dial. The figure four in Roman numerals ought to be written as IV but is always engraved with four wide strokes. This creates a visual balance as the figure eight in the opposite lower position has also four wide strokes in its engraved form. Winding-holes on these late 17th-century dials were plain and sometimes had shutters covering them from behind. Mounted on a pivot, these were moved aside when a maintaining power device was applied, prior to the winding of weight-driven clocks. Shortly before 1700, however, it became fashionable for the winding-rings, the seconds indicator aperture and the calendar box, if circular, to

25 *Above:* A 10″ square dial showing cherub spandrel decorations, an applied seconds ring and well-proportioned chapter ring, by John Williamson of Leeds, circa 1690.

26 *Above right:* An 11″ dial from a long-case clock by Edward Speakman, London, made in about 1710. The chapter ring shows quarter-hour markings and fine half-hour decorations.

27 *Right:* Detail of a dial from a clock by Henry Hindley of Wigan (about 1730), with shutters covering plain winding holes. This feature indicates a clock with bolt-and-shutter maintaining power.

be heavily ringed with turned and polished circles. These formed a pleasing contrast to the matt centre which was textured and rough though bright gilt in finish. The cherub spandrel decorations had additional foliage scrolls added to the tops and sides, and in consequence filled the corners to give a busier look to the whole dial. On the chapter ring half-hour decorations were delightfully engraved, often based on the *fleur de lys* and sometimes a decorative cross pattern. Quarter-hour markings, which occupied the circle at the inner side of the chapter ring and had served to mark the progress of the now-obsolete single hand, persisted and added to the charm of the dial at this particularly beautiful period. Signatures were now engraved between the V and VII and often gave the town or city of origin as well as the name. From this period it is less common to find the name at the base of the dial plate.

Though similar in most respects to those of long-case clocks, the dials of spring-driven bracket clocks frequently had a mock pendulum aperture in the dial centre, beneath the figure twelve. A concave curved slit was cut away from the dial plate and a small patterned disc of brass which was wired to the verge escapement arbor, showed from behind, thus simulating the action of a bob pendulum and showing at a glance that the clock was working. This explanation always seems to me to be curious, as the characteristic busy click of a verge escapement clearly indicates to all but the very deaf that the clock is in working order. Possibly its decorative appeal was important too. Lantern clock dials too changed subtly and the tall slim lines of the early models began to thicken with age. The chapter ring grew broader and became wider than the body of the clock. In some country districts where the lantern clock retained its popularity well into the 18th century, the chapter ring grew extremely wide, out of all proportion to the clock. These were given the name sheep's head clocks – possibly for their bland, numb look when hung on the farm kitchen wall. One hand was usual until the end of the lantern clock period although lantern clocks with minute indications and even a third, musical train are not unknown. These are, however, very rare.

The next major development in dials occurred about 1715-20 when the arched top was added to the dial plate. At first this varied in size. Occasionally an arch was quite deep and wide but more generally the early arches were shallower than later examples. Common on both bracket and long-case clocks from this period, the arch began as a decorative feature and was fully engraved all over, though sometimes containing the clock-maker's name in an engraved cartouche at its centre. This was sometimes supported by a specially cast brass decoration or, instead of the name, a corner spandrel was used with its corner upright in the arch centre. Possibly the first use to be made of the arch was to provide a lever or single hand with which the strike of the clock could be silenced. This is known as strike/silent indicator, from the words with which the backing ring was engraved. Calendar hands or, more rarely, very early moon phase indicators were incorporated into the early arched dial. Subsequent to its introduction makers of most quality clocks began to use the arched dial form, and by now the long-case clock dial had grown to 12″ square plus the arch. Some early clocks were modernised at this date to acknowledge the new fashion and had an arch added to their square dial plates. These added arches were riveted on by means of brass

28 *Above:* A dial of a late London lantern clock by Henry Webster, made in about 1700. The chapter ring extends beyond the width of the dial plate. Temple Newsam House, Leeds.

29 *Above right:* Detail of a cherub spandrel decoration.

30 *Below right:* Detail of spandrel decoration of two cherubs holding a crown. This design dates the decoration to some time after 1705.

reinforcing straps at the back and were used for a variety of purposes, though mainly decorative as an existing clock would already carry its maker's name. It also happened that a maker had some square plates in stock when fashions changed, and these too would have been modernised in the same way. Clocks with early alterations can be found, but they should not be confused with spurious examples altered recently to fit odd clock components into an arch dial case. After a few years the arch settled into a more regular shape and from then until the end of the long-case clock period it was usually about a half-circle in shape. Bracket clocks of the first quarter of the 18th century particularly were likely to differ from the square dial with an arch at the top. Some had tall oblong dials and others had tall oblong dials with an arch. The extra spaces were filled with sub-dials for such purposes as regulating the length of the pendulum, strike/silent calendars and moon phases. If the clock was a musical one, the tune could be chosen by rotating a pointer in the sub-dial. The titles of the tunes were frequently fully engraved around the edges of the ring.

From 1700 some variety is to be expected in the design of the cast spandrel decoration, although there were never a great number of spandrel decorations throughout the entire clock period – possibly about 30 including those used in the arch as well. It is rare to find a new or unique design. Makers and regions appear to have had their favourite designs and stuck to them with infrequent deviations. Like bells and other castings,

43

spandrels were bought in from foundry representations. Following the enlarged cherub spandrel decoration and becoming popular about 1705, was a design featuring two cherubs holding a crown and flanked by foliate scrolls. This is thought to celebrate symbolically the Protestant ascendancy. Similar designs were carved into the front rails and crestings of chairs during the William-and-Mary period. Many Dutch craftsmen were working in the London furniture and clockmaking crafts at this time and their influence on decoration was considerable. Later versions had a larger crown, and generally this design persisted for a long time.

Satyrs and also female heads flanked by foliage scrolls were used at this time as spandrel ornaments. The satyr head was particularly used by good London makers of the beginning of the 18th century. Later into the century, patterns became more numerous and the degree of finish in the casting diminished.

From about 1730, an urn provided a central feature for some spandrel decorations. Many others were produced with foliage only and the rococo period influenced the design by introducing C- and D-scrolls, common in all decorative features of the period about 1770. Three or four variations of this type are known. The later northern brass-dial clock, particularly the Lancashire type, are typified by their use of a large openwork rococo spandrel decoration with an apex scroll resembling a question mark. A late version of the cherub spandrel decoration also occurred in the north from about 1750. A large cherub head with heavy scroll and scallop work characterises this type, which was used until the end of the brass-dial period. A decoration during the mid- and late-18th century, which is not very highly regarded by most horologists, is the set of four corners showing figures symbolising the seasons. This idea was also common on Dutch clocks and carried over into the painted-and white-dial period, when figures representing the seasons were painted into dial corners. Also during the painted-dial period the 'set of four' as a decoration extended to figures in the corners representative of four known continents: normally a Red Indian, a negro African, a Chinese woman, and a European.

Before describing further developments, it is as well to look at the skills involved in making a brass dial. We expect to see the delightful variety of surface on cast and hand finished brass plate until the late 18th century. After this time, when machine-rolled brass plate became a possibility, it was occasionally used. Even then its use was very limited in clockwork. The reverse of a dial plate or chapter ring gives a clear indication of this method of production. It may also render a

31 *Left:* Large open-work rococo spandrel decorations, on which the apex scroll resembles a question mark. The engraving of the dial centre has a similar rococo quality. Long-case clock by Dollif Rollisson, Halton, Leeds, circa 1770. Temple Newsam House, Leeds.

32 *Right:* A north-country dial plate from the rear, showing the gaps left behind the chapter ring.

few clues to the clock's history with inscriptions scratched by repairers, or may show the engraver's trial strokes as he practised the forming of a letter. This is more common in country work. Sometimes too a date or a journeyman's name is engraved in places not normally seen by anyone other than the restorer. A feature found in the dials of clocks made north of the Midlands is the cut-away or, more precisely, cast-away section left in the area of the dial plate covered by the chapter ring. This practice, very likely done for reasons of economy, was the norm in the mid- and later-18th century but was not always carried out on northern clocks of the very early 18th century.

It is often obvious that country makers in isolated places did their own engraving, and on some of those country 30-hour clocks one can see the greatest departures from the normal way of doing things in this highly conservative craft. Imperfections in brass castings leaving pit gaps and sandmarks, thin scratchy engraving, punched decorations, crudely engraved patterns and naively lettered legends and verse often relating to the passage of time and Man's mortality, all add up to the charm of some country 30-hour clocks. Finely engraved dials were clearly the work of a master engraver and when we consider the division of labour that went on in the clockmaker's workshops of any size, it is plain that the clocks were engraved

by one who was a specialist in that field. He may have been an employee of the clockmaker, but most dials were sent out. Throughout the 18th century the engraver was an important and busy craftsman engaged upon engraving printing plates, book illustrations, maps, silver plate and many other items including clock dials which would form his everyday business. It is sometimes suggested that mistakes, for example in the spelling of a clockmaker's name, indicate that the engraving was sent out. However, variety in spelling, even of a name, was not uncommon in those days and an obvious mistake can be made, even of one's own name, when concentrating on the letter form and making a good job of the engraving. From time to time, one also sees a mistake in the numbering. Recently I saw a clock with two 25s engraved in the minute band when the correct figures should have read 20 and 25. Over-concentration probably led to this charming error.

After the introduction of the applied brass chapter ring and sub-dials, it became the norm to provide contrasts of finish by the use of gold, silver and black wax in differing parts.

The dial plate and spandrel decoration of early clocks were nearly always mercurially gilt to give a bright glow, richer looking than polished brass. This was particularly so in the 'golden period' at the end of the 17th century and the beginning of the 18th. The chapter rings and any sub-dial rings pinned on to the dial plate and the calendar ring which revolved on rollers behind the dial plate were given a silvered finish by applying an amalgam of silver chloride paste, salt and

33 Detail of a dial by John Ismay, Oulton, Cumberland, circa 1710. Imperfections in the casting of the metal can be seen on the chapter ring between the hours nine and ten. Simple decoration and scratchy engraving make this a typical early country clock. The hands are a replacement. The movement of this clock is shown in Plate 85.

tartaric acid. Although this produced a silver deposit it did not resemble polished silver, but when correctly done gave a good white finish to the rings. The engraved numerals, which had previously been filled with black wax, showed through and gave a clear and beautiful contrast.

It is very rare to find evidence of the original dial surface on a clock, for this has often been destroyed by active cleaning and polishing of the dial, or has perished by neglect or even age. If exposed to atmosphere silvering, like the solid metal, quickly blackens. When the hands are moved on manually, or catch the ring, or even when the dial is rubbed with a duster, the protective lacquer wears through and the silver coating on the rings deteriorates.

Before moving on to the new fashion for the white- or painted-dial it should be said that for a brief period around 1770-80 dials were made for long-case and bracket clocks which were engraved from a full and plain sheet of brass. These are referred to as a single-sheet dial. Their outline was the same as the conventional dial with applied rings and can be seen in round, arched or square dial form. Corners and sub-dials, as well as hour and minute numerals were all fully engraved. The engraving was filled with black wax and the dial fully silvered, giving a clear black-and-white quality to the finished dial. Many of these dials are admired for their tasteful and restrained style of engraving, and the clarity of the hands when viewed across a room.

By 1772 a startling new departure was made in dial production which led to mass-produced dials to help cater for increased demand for clocks from the growing middle and merchant classes. This was the painted face or white-dial, painted on an iron base or dial plate. Cheapness and speed of manufacture cannot have been an important factor in its introduction for the painting- and number-writing would have taken almost as much time as engraving, and when it was first produced, the white dial was more expensive to produce than the brass dial. It seems possible to account for introduction of the white dial for fashionable reasons alone, for new products were avidly admired then as now. Contemporary advertising lists its advantages, and it is not difficult to imagine that the new white dial was much admired and in great demand. Like the brass dial, the new product went through various stages of development. Contemporary with its introduction came the single-sheet brass dial mentioned above, whose silvered appearance is very similar at first glance; so much so that some authorities feel that the simple style of decoration used on the first white-dials was derived directly from the engraved dial. Others feel that the single-sheet brass dial was introduced by the engraved-dial makers to combat the commercial success of the white-dial. However, which came first is not at issue here. It is enough to say that their design features were both products of the same taste and on the surface they appear very similar indeed. A feature of the earliest white-dials was the simplicty of decoration and the amount of clear white ground which was shown. Decoration was mainly restricted to the spandrels and the edges of the arch, if there was one. This was usually gold rococo work on a raised gesso ground. The black number-writing was delicately done and copied precisely the quality and proportion of the late engraved-brass dial. The maker's name too was written precisely by brush, but in the flowing style of the engraver.

Gradually the dial painters introduced more and more into their dials and areas, such as the dial centre and spandrel corners which had formerly been delicately decorated with swags and scrolls now supported exotic birds, floral bouquets, shells and fans. Less of the white background was left. The trend continued until corners, arches, and sometimes a large part of the dial centre was fully painted. Many dials of about 1830 could even be said to be rather vulgar, and their gaudy colours and brash renderings of such subjects as country cottages, sailing ships, hunting scenes, battle scenes, and pastoral scenes with figures owe more to folk art than the fine craftsmanship shown in earlier white dials.

There had to be some provision for attaching the movement to these new white dials. It had been customary to rivet dial

34 *Left:* A 14″ square white-dial clock signed Barrow, Stockport, about 1790. The false plate fixing is marked Osborne Birmingham; the same firm was also the true dial makers.

35 *Right:* Rear view of the same dial, showing the cast-iron false plate supplied with the dial to enable it to be fixed to the movement.

feet into the old brass dial at any point underneath the chapter ring, once it had been established that the dial feet would not foul the strike work or any other of the motion work of the clock. Carried out in the same workshop that the clock was made, this was an easy job. The new white-dial was factory-made (most of them were made in Birmingham) and also the painted surface could be damaged by later riveting on dial feet, so that a means was introduced to overcome this problem. This was the 'false plate'. Attached to the back of the dial by four very short dial feet, the false plate was an intermediary plate of ample proportion to allow further brass feet which would fasten the false plate to the movement at a convenient point. This meant that the dial's surface was not damaged and all riveting could take place on the removable false plate. Once this problem was removed the only remaining consideration was to see that the movement was designed to match up with the winding holes, seconds-hand hole and date hole or lunette aperture if fitted. Makers using Birmingham dials must therefore have had to buy in a dial and use it to lay out the final placing of clock train before drilling the plates. In eight-day white-dial clocks after 1800 the absence of a false plate can indicate that the clock movement as well as the dial was bought complete by the man whose name appears on the dial. In these cases three dial feet are often used in preference to the more usual four. Thirty-hour clocks, which are wound by pulling on a rope or chain, never had the complication of aligning winding holes with winding squares or the seconds indicator with its hole in the dial. Much of their strike work was placed between and behind the plates of the clock. The false plate was therefore not necessary and in fact they are rarely if ever fitted to an unaltered 30-hour clock, even though Birmingham white-dials were commonly used in their making. Made of cast iron, the false plate adds an additional interest to the clock for nearly all examples were cast with their maker's name. Thus the dial-maker's period of working can be established as well as the clockmaker whose name is on the dial, giving a further guide to dating the clock accurately.

Few artists ever signed the dials they painted. Indeed, of the hundreds of dials that I have handled, only one has been signed by its painter. Since the clock in question is a white-dial, long-case clock by Booth of Pontefract, Yorkshire, made about 1830, and has three dial feet and no false plate, it is quite likely to have been bought in by Mr. Booth from a Birmingham factory. No markings are evident on the dial plate or movement, but the artist has signed the back of the dial plate in such a way that suggests that he always did this, but no others as far as I know have yet come to light. It says clearly and simply:

Schwanfelder

Painter and Clock Dial Enameller

Bottom of Wade Lane, Woodhouse Bar

Leeds.

There is nothing written about the actual painting of clock dials, who did what, and at what stage. It seems to me, from handling and restoring many of them, that the colour-work and the black numerals and signature were often done at different times. It could be that in some cases the coloured pictures or decorations were painted on in the factory, and the black work added later by the clockmaker's local artist, dial writer or, as in the case of the Schwanfelder dial, the whole thing painted by arrangement after the dial left the factory. I make those points as no-one else has recorded that many worn and rubbed dials have lost their black work, when the colour-work still retains much of its original surface. The oil-painted coloured areas are quite heavily protected by varnish, whereas the numerals and signature in black have been carried out in what appears to have been a water-based paint or ink and left unprotected. Over the years washing has removed many of the numbers and frequently the maker's name and town of origin as well.

Bracket clock dials during the late Georgian period changed in the same way as on the long-case clock; the single-sheet silvered brass dial was used by some makers for a time. However, variations never regularly used in long-case work were introduced. French clocks commonly have enamelled dials. That is a true enamel, kiln fired on a copper base, giving a ceramic like hard surface which should not be confused with the painted surface of a white-dial. Never a typical feature of English work, enamelled centre parts such as a chapter ring and dial centre all in one were very occasionally used on an arched brass dial plate and flanked by the traditional cast spandrel decoration. As early as 1760 a bracket clock was made by John Ellicot of London with a simple circular convex enamelled dial. This must have looked particularly plain at this period but we know it to have been a forebear of the circular painted dial style which was almost exclusively used on bracket clocks in the Regency period. The full-coloured pictorial dial was never a feature of bracket-clock work, and during the period 1810-40 it was almost exclusively used on the long-case clock. The painted dial applied to the bracket clock was usually a plain circular product whose main claim to

36 *Opposite above left:* An 11″ dial of a long-case clock by William Tipling of Leeds, circa 1705. The particularly beautiful hands are its finest feature. This is a late example of engraving the signature at the base of the dial plate.

37 *Opposite right:* Fine marquetry month-going long-case clock by William Honeychurch of Rotherhythe, London, circa 1710, with added arch. Judging by the quality of both dial and case this would appear to be an original alteration.

38 *Opposite below left:* Painted arched dial signed Booth, Pontefract. It is signed on the back by the dial painter Schwanfelder. The arch of the dial features a rocking ship, while the lower dial centre shows Brittania pointing upwards to indicate the fate of the dying Nelson. The corner decorations are emblematic of the seasons.

William Tipling in Leeds fecit

BOOTH   Pontefract.

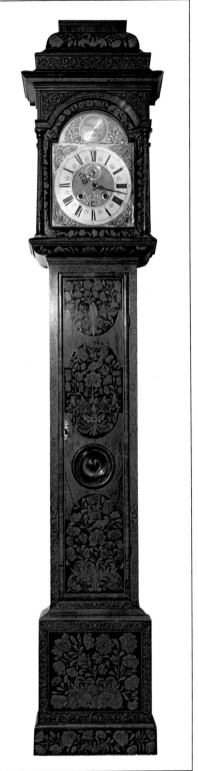

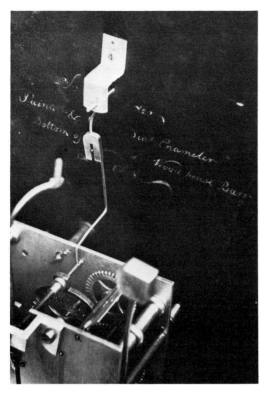

39 *Opposite:* Fine arched dial from a long-case clock by Thomas Dodson of Leeds in about 1780. The curious arch painting depicts soldiers attacking a castle, while a cavalry man rocks in the centre, in the act of cutting down a fleeing foot-soldier. A centre calendar is engraved on the inside of the chapter ring and the dial centre incorporates two sporting scenes.

40 *Left:* Rear of the dial of Plate 38 painted by Schwanfelder and showing the painter's signature and address. The lead-off from the escapement working the rocking ship can be seen.

41 *Right:* A bell-topped bracket clock with a circular enamel dial. Anonymous, circa 1770.

popularity must have been its legibility. These dials too were made by the Birmingham dial-makers and also had a false plate for affixing to the movement. This plate was a full circular sheet, usually of thin tin- or zinc-plate pinned directly to the back of the convex circular dial.

Nothing can spoil the appearance and balance of a clock dial more than ill-considered replacement hands. Rarely was the original clockmaker's choice a poor one when making or fitting hands. Sufficient original examples exist on the correct dials for us to know what is right for any particular period. While the detail and finish varied from clock to clock and workshop to workshop, the design of hands was, like dials and corner pieces, a fairly conservative area and certain shapes, scrolls and loops were expected at certain times. Occasionally a spectacular pair of hands appeared on a dial of a special clock. Such a pair are illustrated in Plate 36 and were made in about 1705 by William Tipling of Leeds for an 11″ square-dial eight-day clock. To appreciate such hands fully it is necessary to know how they were made. A number of skills were necessary and to cover the whole process it is generally said that steel hands were 'wrought'. Viewed from the side the hand generally has a variable thickness, as the first part of the making was to

42 A lantern clock by John Ball of Newport Pagnell, featuring a single hand with oval boss, and a tail to aid setting.

hammer a hot piece of iron so that it was thinned at the tip or decorative part of the hand whilst remaining about $\frac{1}{8}''$ thick at the boss, or part which was attached to the clock. The later the clock and the plainer the hand, the more regular its thickness will usually be. In late 18th-century clocks and some bracket clocks of the 19th century hands were made from a very uniform sheet of metal, shaped only in two dimensions. The shapes and scrolls of the outline would next be drawn or scribed on to the surface of the metal and then cut and pierced into the general shape required. Finishing would be carried out with fine files and the front surface sculptured and engraved at points where scrolls flowed together or met the rounded edge of the hand. This important and skilled work would not be entirely the job of an apprentice, though it is often quoted as an apprentice's job by writers on the subject. Great care is required in the finishing of a hand and this very obvious part of the clock needed a steady and skilled craftsman's touch.

The early domestic clock featured only a single hand. At the beginning of the 17th century and before even lantern clocks became plentiful, a feature of these hands was their thickness and simplicity of construction. They often had a flattened oval shaped boss. The tail, a feature of single hands, aided the owner in setting the clock to time, and was plain and about a third of the length of the main part of of the hand. The tip of the hand terminated in a plain arrow-head shape. Slightly later but still seen in very early clocks was the variation terminating in a blunt fork-shaped hand as illustrated on page 56 (B). These styles were developed and followed by a simple loop pattern with drilled ears at either side of a short blunt point. By this time it had become customary to use a heavy circular boss on all hands; infrequently, but on some high-quality clocks, this was ring turned just inside its outer edge. During the last quarter of the 17th century when verge lantern clocks were made in increasing numbers, the decorative loop-ended hand was made in some variety, although it never became complicated in the same way that long-case clock hands were to become in the early years of the 18th century.

From 1660 or thereabouts two hands were introduced into clockwork, as a result of the development of the pendulum and increased accuracy in timekeeping. At first these were a decorative hour-hand and a much longer and simpler minute pointer. This arrangement persisted for more than a hundred years until matching steel hands became fashionable on early painted dials. The hour-hand which was thus paired up with a minute pointer was at first little more than an elongated lantern clock hand without the tail while the minute-hand was a plain pointer for the final three-quarters of its length, mounted on a base shaped like a small looped S and then the circular boss. A section through the top of this pointer would show that it was filed up to a triangular section, the base of which was nearer to the dial surface.

During the golden period of English clockmaking after about 1680 hour-hands became extremely elaborate and finely detailed. London clockmakers in particular needed to make fine hands to match the engraved surfaces of their beautiful dials. Hour-hands developed into a multiplicity of loops and scrolls and as a result became larger. The decorative portion of some was cone-shaped and rather slim in proportion whereas others were broad with ear-like projections, depending on the preference of the clockmaker in question. Minute pointers, while becoming a little broader at the base remained similar, using the same S shape with individual variations. Seconds pointers used on eight-day long-case clocks from this time were always perfectly plain, being small parallel pointers

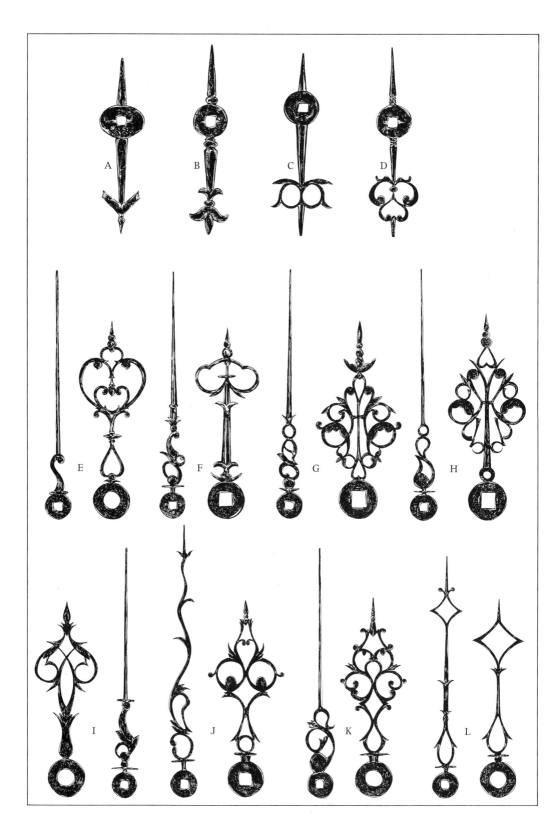

A,B,C,D Lantern clock hands showing their development.
E,F Clock hands from the period 1660-70.
G,H Two pairs of fine clock hands from the 'Golden Period' 1680-1710.
I Cross-over loop pattern found on hour hands after 1750.
J A pair of hands from about 1760-70. The minute hand shows the wavy Dutch pattern.
K A pair of steel hands of a pattern commonly found on provincial dials of 1770-80.
L A pair of matching steel hands of diamond pattern, often used on early white-dial clocks.
M,N Two pairs of brass hands of the type used on the 19th-century white-dial clock, with punched decoration.
O A seconds hand of a plain early type.
P A date pointer of 1760.
Q A seconds hand from a clock by Thomas Ogden of Halifax, circa 1740.
R A date pointer with an unusual curving tail from a white-dial clock of about 1800.
S,T Brass seconds pointers from 19th-century long-case clocks.

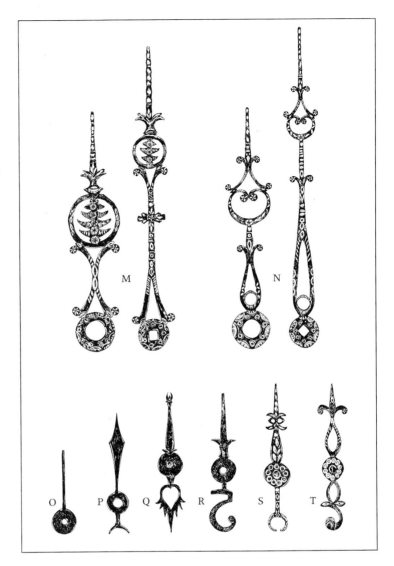

emanating from a round boss. As with the main hands this boss was sometimes ring-turned to add to its decorative quality. In the first three decades of the 18th century hand shape and quality remained very fine. The hour-hand continued with variations of pierced scrolls and loops interspersed with fine straights and strapwork holding together the elaborate design. From the turn of the century, however, a change came about in the design of the minute hand; the base section which had previously been a form of solid S shape was now frequently pierced and scrolled, with a large scroll towards the boss and a smaller one, eccentrically curved towards the plain pointer. Less popular but nevertheless a type of this period was the minute pointer with an S-shaped base, solidly cut with leaf-like projections at either side. Bracket clock hands were exactly the same at these times, but of course on a reduced scale to suit the smaller dials.

A gradual decline in quality and style is noticeable from the middle of the 18th century, although many fine hands were produced on clocks from provincial and country districts as well as London-made clocks. Less detail was generally put into the hour-hands decorative spade and many of them were of a crossover loop pattern, similar in style to the splat of a country Chippendale chair. From this period too the wavy-style minute-hand, which is said to have been a Dutch idea, became increasingly popular. With certain designs repeated and with quality depending more on the individual maker rather than the date or place, these styles carried on into the white-dial period. Later brass or single-sheet engraved dials often had hands that could be interchanged with the first white-dial examples.

Shortly after the introduction of the white-dial, the fashion for matching steel hands came about. These matched in style but were of course proportionally different to suit their differing roles. A well-made hour-hand should just reach the hour circle at the base of the hour numerals and a minute-hand should reach exactly the divisions in the minute band. By 1800 brass clock hands were extremely popular on the Birmingham dials, although special clocks and some fine regulators continued to have simple and functional hands made in steel. As well as an obvious change in material the manner of making the brass hand was also very different. These were almost always pressed or sheared out of sheet brass. The surface decoration which was closely filled with punched patterns was probably also impressed at the same time. It seems likely that these hands were mass-produced in Birmingham and other centres. Many matching patterns were available, from a diamond-shape with crossover loop corners, a crown design, to a Scottish thistle pattern. Many were fine and delicate in their execution, although, as in each preceding style, time broadened their proportions, and towards the end of the long-case clock period they had become quite heavy and ugly in appearance. While seconds-hands with simple tails were not uncommon in the period of steel hands, those made to use with the matching brass hands had heavy curved decorative tails. Few bracket clocks had brass hands and they were in any case never decorated to quite the extent found in long-case work. With the coming of the circular white and enamelled dial, simple hands were preferred, many of them in the French style

43 Unusual use of brass hands on a clock by William Lister of Keighley, circa 1760. The Lister family of clockmakers almost always used heavy brass hands of this type on their brass dials.

made popular by the watchmaking family Breuget.

Special and unusual indications were added to the clock's function by clockmakers at the end of the 17th century in order to impress. Skills were developed to such an extent that clocks could be made to go for twelve months at one winding and to play music, complicated chimes and strike the hours. Astronomical and zodiacal indications were sometimes added and at least one workshop, that of Fromanteel and Clarke of London, showed the moon's phases on their clocks at this early date. All these functions influenced the design of the clock, for selector hands, chime/silent or strike/silent hands, moon and astronomical indications had to be shown on the dial. The first function of the arch in early arched-dial clocks from about 1720 was almost always to house a strike/silent hand. It must have been considered necessary in those days to switch off the strike when going up to bed. It seems then that customer requirements in clocks must have been taken into account. From time to time we see a clock with a very specialised function such as tidal dials or day-of-the-week indicators. One day-of-the-week indicator disc on a rather special year-going long-case clock by Morgan Lowry of Leeds in about 1740 has, under the name of the day, an engraving of the mythical character after whom the

day is named and a date disc showing the year and the Dominical letter, perhaps used by a clergyman in planning his services. By far the most important addition to the clock, however, and regularly seen was a dial indicating the phases of the moon. It may seem a pleasing novelty to us but it was vital in the 18th century. An evening journey would be made at or near a full moon, as highwaymen in the country and footpads in the city were a serious hazard. Plates 44 and 45 show two types of moon dials used through the whole period of long-case clockmaking. They were rarely if ever used in bracket clocks. A solar disc is very rare and usually placed in the arch of the dial, showing the position of the sun in the heavens. It can sometimes be mistaken at first glance for a moon dial, as its arrangement and position is the same. The solar dial is, however, driven directly by gears from the 24-hour wheel in the motion work behind the dial and, unlike the moon dial which revolves every two months, the solar dial revolves every 24 hours, the sun rising to a visible position at 6 a.m. and setting or revolving out of view at 6 p.m. The painted sun is therefore at its highest position at 12 o'clock and at night a dark blue sky is visible on the painted disc. Engraved above on a fixed semicircular rim plate is the position of mid-day in various parts of the world.

Tidal indications were marked in conjunction with a moon

44 *Left:* The most common type of moon dial in the arch of a clock.

45 *Right:* A revolving-ball moon. The moon's age is shown by a hand pointing to the calibrations at the ball moon's centre. This is from a clock by Thomas Ogden of Halifax and is the best and rarest type of moon indicator.

46 Detail of the dial of the eight-day clock by William Bothamley about 1780, showing the tidal indicator carrying information used by cattle drovers in the region of the Wash. The Spalding Gentlemen's Society Museum.

dial and, when this was done, a separate scale showing the local tides was engraved on a ring next to the moon's age. A pointer for each indication was used for whereas the moon's phases are fairly constant, the tides are later by so many minutes each day. The tidal pointer could be set to this difference once it was known. An eight-day clock in the Museum of the Gentlemen's Society, Spalding, Lincolnshire, made by William Bothamley of Kirton in about 1790 shows not only time of day, day of the month and phases of the moon in the arch of the dial, but also points, on a special dial marked with a hand, to the safe and proper time for guides and drovers to start crossing the Wash with their cattle. It is said that the clock was kept in an old inn at Fosdyke and was anxiously consulted by travellers before venturing on to the two miles of shifting sand and the varying channels of the of the estuary. Tidal dial clocks were naturally popular and useful in coastal areas.

Animated or rocking figures are sometimes seen in weight-driven long-case clocks, particularly those made in provincial centres. These occur on both brass and painted dials and are a very attractive novelty, although if badly balanced they play havoc with the timekeeping qualities of the clock. Subject matter for these figures was very varied and among the most popular was a fully rigged sailing ship. Father Time rocking away the seconds with his scythe and hour glass was another

great favourite. Others noted less frequently are a musician whose arm moves to bow his cello, a man sawing wood, a rocking swan, two figures on a see-saw and so on. Very infrequently two figures or moving parts of figures are seen pivoted from the dial and coupled at the back, then worked by the same wire from the escapement arbor. Early examples of these on brass dials, seen from about 1770, were engraved on thin brass plate and appeared in cut-away section of the arch, often backed by a darkened backplate and surrounded by an applied engraved ring bearing a legend *Tempus Fugit*. Later examples used on brass dials were frequently painted. The painted style naturally carried through on to the painted dial and was usually rocked against a painted background on the dial's surface plane, supported on a pivot which passed through a small hole in the dial's arch. Later still a large irregular space was cut into the dial arch and this was backed by a fully painted second arch, held with dial feet. The rocking figure, usually a swan or a ship, appeared between these two, supported from below by a wire from the escapement. This is a dramatic and effective way of presenting the feature as it resembles a proscenium arch.

47 Animated figures on the dial of the musical organ clock by George Pyke, circa 1765, featured on Plates 108 and 123. Temple Newsam House, Leeds.

Chapter 4

Clock cases

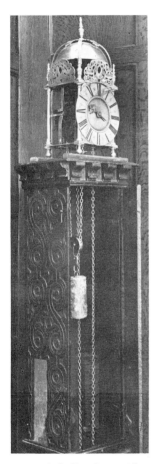

48 Simple hollow base with a door made for the support of a lantern clock. This may date from the late 17th century. Towneley Hall Art Gallery and Museum, Burnley.

In books written until fairly recently, much is said about early cases and indeed of all London clocks before 1700. Later clocks, particularly those made in provincial centres after 1750, have been given very little regard and are often dismissed as being ill-proportioned and of inferior quality. Recent work has shown that many fine clocks were made by craftsmen working all over the country, and beautiful, well-proportioned cases made from fine woods can be found at all periods.

Opinions differ, but the truth is that no-one knows how the first wooden cases for clocks came about. Their arrival in the true and recognised long-case form occurred at the same time as the introduction of the pendulum control from Holland, about the year 1658. Other wooden items such as shelves, hood and tubes on which lantern clocks stood, had existed for many years before this time. It seems likely that the long wooden case was developed simultaneously in various centres, perhaps sometime during the 16th or early 17th century, in an effort to protect the hanging weights from interference by domestic animals, children or others who might otherwise stop the clock. Hollow oak topless cases exist, on which lantern clocks stood, their weights descending into the trunk and out of view. These were a step in the direction of the totally enclosed wooden case. Naive and primitive oak cases which fully enclosed lantern clocks and single-handed country 30-hour clocks are known from the late 17th century. They were also made by country craftsmen until the late 18th century and so give no guide as to the main development in clock-case making.

Plates 18 and 19 show two clocks made about 1680 and illustrate the fine London-made clock case and the simple, honest country product in solid oak.

From the outset the first London long-cases were complete and sophisticated products, made from the finest woods and embellished with gilt metal mounts. They were architectural in style, usually made from oak and veneered in ebony. The very narrow trunk allowed only for the fall of weights, for the pendulum was about 9″ long. Case doors and sides were

A Ebony veneered case made 1660-70.

B Parquetry case of 1670-80.

C Bird-and-flower marquetry case of the Dutch type, 1680-90.

D All-over marquetry case sometimes known as seaweed marquetry, about 1710-15. From 1700 a concave moulding under the hood was usual.

E Walnut case of the London type, circa 1725-40.

F Provincial oak case, mid-18th century.

G Provincial case displaying elements of the Sheraton and Adam styles, using mahogany as the principal wood, circa 1790.

H Mahogany case with a brickwork base of the type favoured in the Liverpool area, circa 1780-90.

I A London mahogany case. The corner columns are reeded with brass at their lower ends, circa 1780-90.

J North-country white-dial clock case. Its principal wood is oak but it is strung and cross-banded with various woods; circa 1800-20.

K Scottish mahogany case with shaped trunk and carved top to the door.

L Yorkshire clock case with diminutive door and wider proportions, but made in exquisite woods, circa 1840-50.

panelled or the veneers were beaded round to give the appearance of panel construction. The hood was made to rise in order to give access to the movement, and was attached to the back board of the case by tongues and grooves which allowed for upward movement. Once raised, a metal catch stopped the hood from falling down. A latch held the hood secure when closed which, because of its shape, was known as a spoon. To open this one only had to open the case door and as this would normally be kept locked no unauthorised person could interfere with any part of the clock. Hoods did not have doors yet.

At either side of the dial aperture and closely attached were plain pillars with brass bases and capitals. The capitals, of Corinthian style, were castings finely finished, gilt and built up from various pieces. Side glasses in the hood gave a view of the movement and became a regular feature of good London casework, certainly until 1740-50. The cases were small compared with later products. A plain base was usually supported on turned bun feet, but many have been damaged and restored since feet of all types of old furniture have been damaged by hard use and damp floors. Only reaching 6 ft or so from the ground, the portico tops of these clocks often had a metal mount in the triangular space of the pediment. This was

E F G H

I J K L

usually a draped swag with a central garland or something similar. A convex moulding in the shape of a quarter-circle under the hood is an indication of a clock of the 17th century. This is a reliable pointer when dating a case, for the practice seems to have stopped after about 1700, when a concave moulding was introduced and became popular. From their design and excellence in construction it is obvious that from the earliest times London cases were the work of men who specialised, within the cabinet-making trade, as clock case-makers. Since they did not sign their work and few records exist, they are unfortunately an anonymous group. One man did, however, leave his mark, in the shape of a token which remained in a specially-made cavity in the base of the case. This has been discovered during restoration and so Joseph Clifton became the earliest recorded English casemaker. The case was made for a clock by Ahasuerus Fromonteel and other cases made for the most important clockmaker of this period have also been seen to bear the same casemaker's style.

The 'architectural' style was brief, for with developments in clockwork and the introduction of the long pendulum changes in case design were necessary. The ebonised case had previously housed a dial of 8″ to 9″ square and was only slightly wider in the trunk. The larger pendulum needed a larger space in which to complete its arc and so cases became wider, and possibly to retain good proportions the size of the dial also increased to 10″ square. Walnut was the wood favoured, used as a veneer on the oak carcase though the very earliest long-pendulum clocks still came within the ebonised, portico-topped period of casemaking. It is worth noting that in some examples the term ebonising refers not only to veneering with ebony, which is a very rare and expensive wood, but also to the application of pearwood or similar fruitwood veneers stained black and making a very good copy of the real thing. Three important changes also took place in the detailing and by 1680 these had become standard features in the design of the walnut case. The hood became flat-topped, surmounted by a frieze of pierced fretwork, backed by silk or similar material and a simple moulding. Barley-sugar-twist columns were used. These were cut from the solid and ebonised to contrast with the rich colour of the walnut hood. A glass lenticle or window was provided in the case door opposite the pendulum bob. This made an attractive feature in the long door and was also useful for it showed at a glance whether the clock was going. These lenticles were large at first and could be circular or oval; eight-sides ones are rare but not unknown. The glass was usually

49 Bird-and-flower marquetry on a month-going long-case clock by Peter East, London, circa 1690. The hood pillars and the plinth to the base are not original. Temple Newsam House, Leeds.

plain, but bulls-eye glass with its green tint was also used. Undoubtedly this provided the most pleasing and decorative look as it distorted and obscured the view of lines and the case backboard, while at the same time the pendulum's glint makes an attractive kaleidoscope. A brass or wooden bezel was used to edge this feature. The wooden ones were polished or gilded; some were ebonised. A few cases from the brief experimental period in the 1670s when pendulums were not a standard length can be seen with a glass lenticle in the base of the case. This indicates that the clock was equipped with a $1\frac{1}{4}$-seconds pendulum, some 61″ long; but these are very rare.

Case doors were large, and in fact took up the whole frontal area of the trunk. They were plain and straight-topped, surrounded with a beaded edge that overhung the dimensions of the door.

In line with other items of furniture at this time, veneered walnut clock cases showed a distinct progression in style. In Restoration times many Dutch craftsmen were employed in England and their massive influence can be seen in the use of parquetry designs in the 1670s and later bird and flower marquetry in the 1680s in panels on the main parts of the case such as the trunk and base. Borders were cross-banded in walnut veneer, and the whole laid on a purpose-built oak carcase. Various woods were used to make veneers for marquetry work and some were stained to give unexpected colours such as green. The edges of a piece in the marquetry design might be burnt in hot sand to give a contrasting dark-shaded edge, and so enhance the sense of drawing in the designs. Mouldings which could not be veneered were made in walnut pieces with the grain laid across the width of the mould. These were glued on to an oak backing piece before being shaped by the moulding plane. This characteristic style is known as cross-grained moulding and is a distinct feature of the walnut period.

By the 1690s marquetry work on clock cases had reached a high level and all-over designs of the so-called seaweed marquetry covered the cases in delicate arabesque designs. This was considered to be a truly English style and was far more delicately executed than the relatively crude Dutch-inspired work of the previous decade. Marquetry was cut from sheets of differently coloured veneers while cramped together, and identical work has been found on two cases which indicates the marquetry was cut at the same time.

While these developments were taking place, clock cases also grew taller to suit the higher plaster-ceilinged interiors of

50 Detail of the base moulding of a walnut long-case clock showing the character of cross-grain moulding.

67

the town houses of the day. With this, dial sizes increased to 11″ and case trunk width also increased in proportion, but generally no more than an inch wider than the dial. Also from this time it became usual for the clock hood to slide forward, and a door was made in the hood for winding and setting the hands. A cushion top was added above the moulding of the hood, often flanked by two or three plinths surmounted by brass ball, or ball-and-spire finials. Some clocks had turned wooden ball finials which were finished with gesso and gilded. This also added to the clock's height. If a marquetry case was not required then the wood used would be well-figured walnut, veneered and crossbanded in just the same way, but with choice burr veneers used on trunk, door and base. Thomas Tompion was known to favour a plain veneered walnut case throughout the marquetry period. On some of these cases the veneers were arranged in the method known as 'oyster shell' parquetry, after their similarity in appearance to that species. The veneers were cut as a section across a small branch, its annular rings giving the irregular circular design. Both olive wood and walnut were used to make the oyster pieces.

51 *Left:* A bird-and-flower marquetry panel, from the case door of the month-going clock illustrated in Plate 37.

52 *Opposite left:* Country long-case clock by William Noke, Bridgnorth, about 1740.

53 *Opposite right:* Walnut long-case clock by William Troutbeck, Leeds, about 1725. The trunk and door are unusually long and the base is shallow, though showing no signs of having been cut down. The clock hands are not original.

54 *Left:* Superb walnut year-going long-case clock by Morgan Lowry, Leeds, circa 1740. Abbey House Museum, Kirkstall, Leeds.

55 *Above:* Large red lacquer musical bracket clock by John Hodges, circa 1735. Temple Newsam House, Leeds.

Provincial makers in cities throughout the country must have ordered cases from London makers, for occasionally one comes across a high quality walnut- or marquetry-cased clock in original and unaltered condition by such a clockmaker. There are also lesser cases with marquetry more sparsely arranged and not so well carried out which are presumably the work of provincial cabinet makers. From 1720 there was an increasing number of country clocks with solid oak cases. These were of both the 30-hour and eight-day duration; many of these were nicely made and echo the proportions and style of more sophisticated London clocks.

Lacquer cases decorated in the oriental manner began to appear in England in the last 20 years of the 17th century. Oriental furniture had been imported in small quantities since the reign of Elizabeth I but the flamboyant tastes of the Restoration provided for its popularity. Opinions differ about whether cases were made in England and sent on the long sea voyage to the East for lacquering or whether they were lacquered in England in imitation of the oriental style. Early in this period of popularity some cases were undoubtedly sent to the East but most were made and decorated in London to oriental recipes and designs. The pictorial parts of the design were raised up in a gum-based gesso and then gilt with details drawn in by brush. This was backed by an overall coloured lacquer ground. Colours were mainly dark; blues, greens and black and more rarely red, yellow and a paler turquoise blue were used. In bracket clocks lacquering did not enjoy the same popular appeal as on the long-cases. At the same time the lacquer artists were well known for their imitation of tortoise-shell and marble effects used successfully on bracket clock cases. The carcase wood for cases was more usually oak but occasional high-quality lacquer clocks were made from pine. This taste for lacquer spanned the period from the square dial to the beginning of the arched dial clock about 1720. The art was taken up by amateurs who were said to lacquer many unsuitable pieces of furniture of all types; the style flourished and then by 1730 lost its appeal.

Later in the 18th century lacquering again became popular for long-case clocks. The carcase wood at this time was invariably oak and the shape of the cases was generally that typical of the pagoda-style hood or round-topped mahogany clock of this period. The fashion lasted for about ten years and died out finally in about 1780.

In their *Treatise of Japaning and Varnishing* (1688) J. Stalker and G. Parker claimed that 'no damp air, no moulding worm or corroding time, can possibly deface the work'. Many cases which survive are distinctly shabby now and unlike polished wood they are difficult to renovate successfully. Consequently they have been less than popular with collectors in recent years.

Towards the middle years of the 18th century London clockmakers were not called upon to make so many long-case clocks. Portable or bracket clocks and clocks fulfilling a special need, such as precision regulators for observatory or similar work, continued to be made, with some fine domestic long-case clocks later on in the mahogany period around 1760-90. The emphasis of case development from this period onwards therefore shifts from London to provincial centres and from specialist clock-case makers to cabinetmakers and country joiners who made all manner of things from breakfront bookcases to coffins. The factor in deciding its style depended not entirely on when it was made as where it was made and by whom. Geographical differences made quite a number of variations in the interpretation of a nationally used style, and an expert can begin to say what part of the country a piece was made by looking at the case alone.

By far the most common wood used for provincial cases was oak. From the early 18th century this was used on its own, relying on the decorative rays of its grain in quarter-cut form for case doors, base panels and so on. From about 1740 cross-banding was popular and, in common with other country-made pieces of furniture, this was applied to the edges of doors and base panels in bands varying in width from $\frac{1}{2}''$ to 2''. The veneer used in banding was usually mahogany although walnut is not unknown. Cases made in this later style might have had a backboard in oak, but deal was equally common. Mahogany is not generally thought to have been used in furniture-making until after the mid-18th century; 1760 is the date usually given. Robert Gillow, a joiner and cabinetmaker and founder of the important firm of Gillows of Lancaster, is recorded as making 'a clockcase of mahogany' in 1743. The firm went on to produce many more fine clockcases in mahogany, oak and pine during the 18th century, and has left us a unique record of their work in ledgers, estimate books and drawings. Plate 57 shows the handwritten estimate for a mahogany long-case and Plate 58 the design and measurements for the case.

The better-quality mahogany cases were those using choice mahogany veneers glued on to an oak carcase. Mouldings and cornices were made from the solid and occasionally

56 *Above:* Country oak case of a one-handed clock by Jeremy Spurgin, Colchester, of about 1695.

57 *Opposite:* Estimate for a mahogany long-case from one of Gillows' handwritten estimate books.

Mahy ... Cupboard ... wood in ... with white

June ye 19th 1788 — a Clockcase with arch'd Face Mahy (323)

2 3/4 ft of 1 Inch Mahy and Birch Ven the door at 1/10 Pft		5 0 1/2
2 1/2 ft of 1 Inch Oak and Birch Ven and Kingwood do the Pedistall front	at 1/6 Pft	3 9
10 1/2 ft of 1/2 Inch Mahy Sides of Body Head and Pedistall	at 7d Pft	6 1 1/2
9 1/2 ft of 1 Inch Mahy Mouldings Pillers Columns and Part of front and Glass frame &c	at 1/2 Pft	11 1
2 ft of 1 Inch deal. Mahy and Kingwood Ven a Part of the Head	at 1/ Pft	2 0
1 1/4 of 1/2 Inch Part of the Glass frame		7 1/2
1 3/4 ft of 1/4 Inch Mahy	at 4d Pft	7
9 3/4 ft of 1/2 Inch Oak the Back of do	at 2 3/4 Pft	2 2 1/2
3 1/2 ft of 1/2 Inch and 1/4 Inch deal	at 1 1/4 Pft	4 1/4
1 Lock Escutchion and Hinges		1 10
1 Pair of Swan Neck Hinges and Ring for Glass door		3
2 Pair of Corinthian Caps and Bases		5 4
Turning the Columns Caps and Bases and Mouldgs		2 4
1 Sheild and 2 Roses for do		2 6
Glew Oil wax Nails and Incidents		2 10
Makeing do Christn Procter	~~Compleate~~	2 .. 0 ..
Glass for the door in the Head		.. 4 ..
	£4	0 .. 00 .. 10 1/4

June ye 19th 1788 a Bracket for a Bust or Vase

2 ft of 5/8 Inch Mahy	at 7d Pft	1 2
1 ft of 1/2 Inch Mahy	at 6d Pft	6
Mahy Ven for the Rim Glew'd up in three		4
a Peice of Mahy for a Block in the top of do		2
3 Brass Holdfasts and Screws for do		3
Makeing do Thos Romney	2 days	.. 4 .. 0
Glew Oil and Incidents		.. 2 ..
	£	.. m ..
a Case to Pack do 8 1/2 ft of 1/2 Inch deal at 1 1/4 Pft		10 1/2
Trunk Nails		1 1/2
Makeing do and Packing 1 Hour		1 9 0

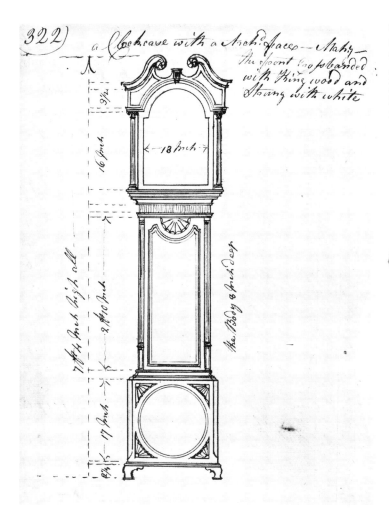

322) *a Clockcave with a Arch'd faces — Mahy —*
the front Crossbanded
with thing wood and
Strung with white

58 *Left:* Drawing with measurements relating to the estimate shown in Plate 57.

59 *Below:* Cuban mahogany long-case clock by John Hawthorn, Newcastle, circa 1780.

used the cross-grained style for effect, but straight-grained mouldings were more usual. Flame or feathered designs could be achieved by matching veneers cut from the same piece of wood and arranging them symmetrically side by side. Mahogany cases of this type tend to be in the dark rich wood known as Cuban mahogany, as much of it was imported from there. Probably one reason for its early use by Gillows is that it would have been imported into Liverpool, an important port trading with the Caribbean at that time. When used in the solid, mahogany never seemed to have been worked with the same kind of flair, and most used wood with unexciting grain and paler colour known as bay-wood or Honduras mahogany. Late 18th-century cases made for both the brass and enamelled dial frequently displayed features common to the designs of Hepplewhite and Sheraton, particularly boxwood stringing, design of cornices, circular and oval outlines to veneered

60 A mahogany veneered white-dial clock by William Jackson of Workington. Boxwood stringing is used as decoration and the pediment of the hood is faced with blue glass with gilt decoration.

panels and the delicate splayed feet (known as French feet) of certain heavy white-dial clocks. Many mahogany cases at this period used a combination of thinly cut solid mahogany planks and mahogany veneers backed with pine in their carcase construction.

Many country-made clocks particularly of the 30-hours winding type with both brass and painted dials were originally housed in pine cases. These were almost always of a plain construction and shape. Flat tops were most usual but a simple version of any regional style of top can be expected.

It is currently fashionable for some antique dealers to strip and polish pine cases, leaving the wood with an exposed grain and its pale natural colour. This was never the original intention of the casemaker, who would have variously had them painted or scumbled and grained to resemble a darker and more expensive wood. Fittings used with pine cases and occasionally on less expensive country oak cases were commensurately cheaper. Instead of a small lock and key for the trunk door, a simple turn-buckle fastening was used. This was turned from the outside of the door by a simple brass ring.

The feature which most characterises the difference in case shapes is generally the hood and its decorative treatment above the dial. The hood A on page 76 is the most common shape for country work with square dials, and with minor differences was made in all regions. Side pillars to the hood could be either attached to the glazed door or separately fixed, as they were in most northern examples. Fixed pillars were most likely to have wooden turned capitals and bases finished in gesso and gilt. Separate pillars were attached to the hood by brass caps and bases. These were fastened with small brass nails to the horizontal parts of the hood. Drawing B is a development of this style with a built-up cushion or caddy top. In the example shown here this has been further heightened with another phase surmounted by a spire finial, from an eight-day clock of some quality with a solid oak case of about 1740 by James Woolley of Codnor in Derbyshire.

The swan-necked or horned pediment was another style to enjoy inter-regional popularity, but it was in the north that it was used most. Many inexpensive square-dial clocks were made in this manner, but with the popularity of the arched white-dial clock the style came into its own and 90 per cent of these clocks were housed in cases with hoods like drawing D. Another elaboration of this basic style is seen on high-quality mahogany cases by some clockmakers in the north-west of England and a type which is generally thought to be

A Square-topped hood with simple moulding. This is the most common shape for country work.

B A more sophisticated variation of A, with a cushion top.

C Hood with square aperture and horned pediment.

D Hood with arched aperture and horned pediment. This was a common style for north-country white-dial clocks.

E Over-elaborate hood of the type used on mahogany clocks in the late 18th century made in the north-west of England.

F Hood with a broken-arch pediment. Although fairly rare, this type is often associated with a round dial.

G Hood with broken-arch top.

H Arched-top hood. This type had a few variations.

I Pagoda-topped hood. This example shows the more sophisticated type; less well-proportioned examples are also to be found.

J Arched-top hood with whale's tail cresting.

K Scottish hood, usually found with an arched white-dial.

L Mahogany hood of a Scottish clock, with round dial.

made by Gillows of Lancaster because of the occurrence of certain features. These include the built-up box section behind the swan neck pediment, an exaggerated cushion mould or a heavy central plinth surmounted by decorative finials. Underneath the curving forms and forming the pediment proper are glass panels, usually a rich blue decorated with gold painted scrolls and foliage. The supporting pillars, usually reeded, may come in pairs either side of the hood but more usually they are single separate pillars with high-quality brass capitals and bases. This style is illustrated by drawing E. Circular decorations or paterae decorated the terminal scroll of the horns and these could be made in various ways.

Early clocks of the brass dial era were likely to have cast brass paterae finished in gilt. Later clocks, forming the majority under consideration, had stamped out brass paterae which were finished in gilt or simply polished and lacquered. Simple ring-turned wooden paterae were occasionally used, while on high-quality clocks various innovations have been seen. Thomas Ogden of Halifax on a clock similar to drawing F used a pair of lion's-mask paterae, which when cleaned proved to be a gilt finish on solid lead. Cases by Gillows of Lancaster are frequently seen with paterae carved in high relief from mahogany in the shape of roses. One of the styles of hood least often seen in later work is the architectural, broken-pediment style; although a similar top has been used in some fine work by Justin Vulliamy, the London clockmaker, at the end of the 18th century. It is seen also from time to time in northern clocks. The mouldings which form the top of the broken pediment being decorated in true architectural style with a dentil course. The broken pediment is also used in conjunction with round dials. Although unusual in long-case work they are sometimes found on clocks made in the Sheffield and Derbyshire area. Very similar but with a rounded profile is the broken-arched style shown in drawing G. On some simple renderings this can also look like an ill-formed and incomplete horned top but the better versions with deep-cut top moulding can be very pleasing. It is one style used nationally but seen infrequently, which suggests that it was not popular in its day. Two Leeds-made clocks known to me have hoods in this manner and their styles of construction and choice of oak suggest that they are both by the same casemaker. One of them illustrated here (Plate 61) in a plain unstrung oak case is by Henry Gamble of Bramley, Leeds, and dates from about 1770. The domed or arch-shaped top generally denotes a brass dial clock, since white dials are rarely found in a case of this style. The broken arch was used from an early date and occasionally for high-quality cases in the era of walnut about 1730. In these examples, and London ones made in the later mahogany period of 1760-80, the moulded arch surmounts a delicately fretted frieze. The style was also used early in the 18th century on well-made provincial eight-day clocks. The curved top mould in these examples was either built up in blocks and then veneered in the cross-grained manner or shaped and carved from the solid in the case wood, usually oak. Drawing H on page 76 is a hood made up in exactly this manner. Other hoods of the same design were made in southern counties, East Anglia and northern England – a particularly fine example with a walnut-veneered top-moulding is recorded by John Burgess of Wigan in about 1730. A delicate version of this style was also used on high-class London regulator clocks by makers such as Thomas Mudge and Thomas Dutton. These clock cases were made in fine well-figured mahogany and were austere in their general outlines, relying on the simplicity of line and the figure of the wood for decorative effect. In the view of many people these are among the most pleasing cases ever made.

The whale's tail cresting added to an arch-topped hood gives a completely different character to the clock and is also an interesting regional characteristic (drawing J). It was popularly used by makers in the west country. The Somerset casemaker, Isaac Nichols, made some fine clocks using cases decorated in this way.

In the same way that long-case clocks of north-western England were typified by the swan-necked top and the majestic mahogany case in the late 18th century, the east coast of England was similarly seen to have a style of its own. The styles were not entirely exclusive to each region, for while it is common to see a pagoda-topped case on a clock made on the Yorkshire coast, it is equally common to find one made in Ipswich or even Kent. This was also a style favoured by some London makers for mahogany- and lacquer-cased clocks at the close of the 18th century. The better mahogany case of this type was likely to have brass inserts to the reeding, half way up from the base of the hood pillars. The pagoda top has, in common with all styles, many variations and interpretations. The better clocks resemble closely the tall shape illustrated by drawing I, but shallower, less-understood versions were used in some country districts.

In the pediment at the top of the hood two main types of treatment are found. A cut-away portion echoing the outline of

61 Broken-arch topped eight-day clock by Henry Gamble, Bramley, circa 1770.

62 Shallow pagoda-topped hood on a black and gold lacquered long-case clock by Robert Cutbush of Maidstone, Kent, circa 1740.

the hood would be fitted with a decorative fret cut in a curving loop pattern or occasionally with a geometric fret in the Chinese taste. This backed with silk or something similar, would serve to let out the sound of the bell, but its true purpose was decoration. Marquetry inlay was frequently used in small pointed oval panels at this point on the hood, and also on the trunk door, beneath the hood moulding on the trunk and in the hood frieze, on particularly fine mahogany examples. The subject of these inlays varied but the main ones are the cornucopia and the star-shape fan typified by the work of Robert Adam in his interiors of this time. Oak examples of this style exist in some numbers, and when well chosen and nicely shaped they look well in an undecorated form.

In a book of English clocks it may be inappropriate to mention Scottish cases, but they are so frequently seen south of the Border that all must be dealt with if only for purposes of identification. Nearly all Scottish cases are in the later phase of mahogany, using solid wood with no distinct figure; but exceptions are occasionally seen. I know of no Scottish white-dial clock case made with oak as its principal wood. The hood may look unusually top-heavy. Many hoods such as that in drawing K have a great deal of plain wood above the dial top. The pillars do not always just flank the glassed door but sometimes rise almost to the top mould, giving a distinctly odd appearance to the clock which is at first glance often hard to identify. These pillars may be plain, reeded, or even twisted in style and this can add to the unsuitability of their proportion and presentation. I hope that I may be forgiven for describing the style as distinctly numb in appearance. From time to time one sees a much more delicate style of Scottish long-case. Dating from 1780 onwards, these are usually quite delicate and whimsical in silhouette, and are made from good, well-figured mahogany. Hoods are generally variations on the style shown in drawing L; trunk doors may be shaped or decorated with carved wooden relief towards the top. On occasions the trunk sides may even be tapered or have an entasis which fits in with the whimsical and interesting appearance.

With the increased number of clock cases made by local craftsmen in town and country areas as the 18th century progressed, the frequency of maker's labels also increased, although to find one is an unusual experience. Information about the maker may also be found recorded in pen on the carcase wood of the case. I have seen two examples of this, one written underneath the seatboard of the movement and another recording the clockmaker and the first owner, written

in ink on the edge of the hood door. The label illustrated on Plate 63 is from the backboard of the eight-day clock by Thomas Wilson of Spalding (Plate 64) dated to about 1830 by its style. It is a pleasing later case, finished with well-figured mahogany veneers; the following facts are recorded about the two makers involved. Charles Oliver, the casemaker, disappeared from local trade directories by 1842. A press notice announcing the sale of the jewellery business of Thomas Wilson 'before leaving England' appears in 1849. These contemporary records show that both men were in a position to have done this work in 1830 and so confirm our dating, which was initially made on stylistic grounds.

The spreading outlines of the north country long-case clock in the 19th century have been responsible for the criticism levelled at them by clock connoisseurs over the years. However, it must be said that the workmanship and woods used in their construction were never better. On their surfaces can be seen the choicest mahogany veneers, inlays of rosewood, boxwood and sections of marquetry in satinwood, while stringing in boxwood is a common feature. Gilded patterns were sometimes used on the surface of the veneers in places such as the frieze under the hood moulding of the trunk and also on the hood frieze above the dial. Pillars in the hood were sometimes built up of a sandwich of different coloured

63 A clock-maker's label pasted inside on the backboard of the clock by Thomas Wilson of Spalding (Plate 64). Nail holes can be seen where the clock has at some time been fixed to the wall. Museum of Lincolnshire Life, Lincoln.

64 Mahogany veneered case, circa 1830, made by Charles Oliver of Spalding, for a clock by Thomas Wilson. Museum of Lincolnshire Life, Lincoln.

woods before turning. These would be bobbin-turned, balister-turned or even cut with a heavy spiral twist. Usually quarter-pillars adorned the front corners of the trunk flanking the door, which over the years became smaller and smaller until it was a disproportionate vestige of its former self. Its diminished size also hindered its function, as you will know if you have ever tried reaching inside to put on a weight. The trunk corner pillars are a typical but not exclusive feature of north-country work. This style is also found on other country-made pieces of furniture such as dressers, cupboards, chests and drawers from the mid-18th century. Capitals and bases were turned in the same wood, usually mahogany, for this wood was used even when the pillars were to go on a basically oak piece. On occasions a better case might have brass capitals and bases. When cases originated from the Birmingham area, where foundry work was one of the local trades and castings were more plentiful, the capitals would generally be of the Corinthian type, elaborate and well finished.

Brick-work bases, arranged in mahogany veneer so that the front corners of the base looked like the corner construction of a house, were a common feature on some cases made in the north-west. The style is thought to be a feature of some of Gillow's work. The feature is generally called a Liverpool base since clockmakers in that region favoured cases in this style.

Bracket clocks were never produced in great numbers in country districts or indeed in any centres outside London. A number were made in the south, and some examples were made in East Anglia and the west country. In the north, however, bracket clocks are a distinct rarity. Personally I cannot recall seing one example made in Lancashire. As a result, a discussion of bracket clocks must centre upon London-made cases. The standard was almost always high. Country versions generally adhered to the prevailing style in London and indeed many cases may have been bought in from London casemakers.

Few bracket clocks did actually stand on wall brackets. Those that did are usually of a very late date and few original brackets survive. In fact these clocks were designed for occasional carrying and intended for use on the side table of the drawing room or at night in the bedroom, where the repeating mechanism could be used to indicate the hours and the quarters in the dark. Consideration was also given to their use on the mantelpiece, standing in front of a glass overmantel or mirror; the glass backdoor of the clock allowed a view of the elaborately engraved backplate to be reflected into the room. Bracket or mantel clock cases were at first so similar in style to

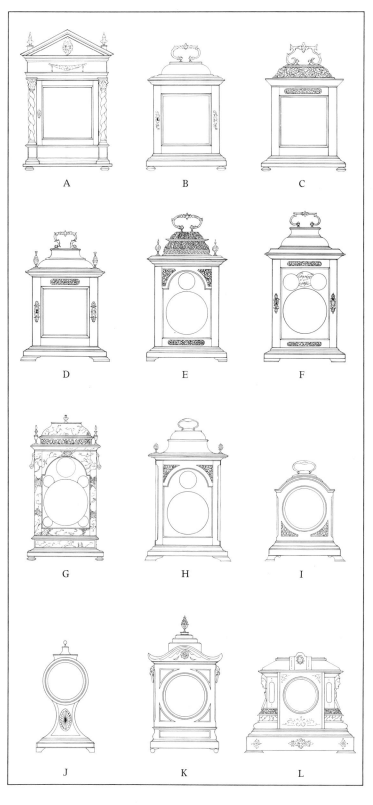

A Architectural-topped bracket clock case with elaborate metal mounts, circa 1665.

B A cushion-topped case with carrying handle, circa 1675.

C Square-dialled case with metal basket-top and elaborate carrying handle, circa 1680.

D Inverted bell-topped case, circa 1710.

E Early arch-dial case with elaborate metal basket-top, circa 1715.

F Case for clock with oblong dial. This also has an inverted bell top and carrying handle.

G Lacquer case with arch-dial aperture and side handles, circa 1740.

H Bell-topped case with plain carrying handle and brass bracket feet.

I Mahogany case for a clock with round dial, circa 1780.

J Balloon-shaped case with circular dial aperture and parquetry medallion, circa 1790-1800.

K Regency case with an oriental flavour but featuring more typically a pineapple top finial and lion's-mask carrying handles at either side.

L Black marble case of the Victorian period.

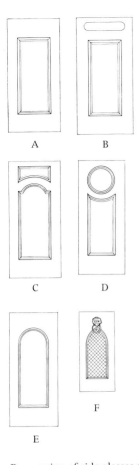

A

B

C

D

F

E

Progression of side glasses of bracket clocks:

A Simple oblong glazed aperture, circa 1670.

B Oblong-glazed aperture with round-ended fret above, circa 1680-1710.

C With the introduction of the arch-dial, side glasses echoed the arch shape, and the fret was given a concave base line; 1715-70.

D A side glass with a concave top and a circular fret. This style is associated with the bell-topped case, 1760-80.

E The shape of the side glass and fret were now combined. It might be filled with either glass or a wooden fret; circa 1780-1800.

F Gothic side fret. This was usually made in fretted brass and backed with silk.

the long-case that they looked exactly like the hoods of the tall clocks. Both portico and flat tops were used and the cases at these dates did not have the top carrying handle. From the 1670s a shallow cushion top was used on cases and the carrying handle was introduced. Ebony and ebonised pearwood veneers on bracket clock cases persisted long after they had become unfashionable on long-cases, and in fact they are not unusual on bracket clocks as late as 1770 when mahogany was the most popular wood for clock cases. Some exotic features were used on the better table clocks which never found their way on to long-case work. Metal basket tops in the shape of a bell were finely cast and chased. In some rare examples these were made of silver, but generally they were finished, along with finials and other brass mounts, in mercury gilt. The dramatic red and black veneers of tortoiseshell were sometimes used. Marquetry, kingwood and walnut were used as an alternative to the usual ebonised surface. Side glasses as well as glass doors, back and front, give an all-round view of the beautiful movements. Escutcheon plates on the front doors were balanced at either side, one for the key hole and one remaining blank. Small pierced frets were let into the tops of the doors and above the case side glasses. About 1″ deep and round-ended they were cut from a thin piece of ebony veneer and backed with silk in the usual way. Pierced basket tops were lined with silk to give a pleasing look and to keep out the dust. Areas of fretwork increased as the time went on. With the introduction of the arched dial in about 1715, the spandrel areas at the top of the door were usually filled with a suitable fretted design. From this period too, the fretwork above the side glasses tended to be shaped in sympathy with the arched side glass, and later on, with the bell-topped style of case, became circular above a concave top to the glass. This is clearly shown by the diagrams on this page. After 1780 it was fashionable to run the two shapes together and fill the total area with either fretwork or glass. Regency and Victorian bracket clocks are typified by brass side frets in a fish-scale design.

As the tops of the cases became higher and more decorative, the carrying handle was magnificently scrolled and finished, until about 1700 it slowly became more simple in its outline. Sometimes a heavy, elaborate clock such as drawing G, in the illustrations of bracket clock cases on page 82, had no handle at all. A departure from the basic shape, which had persisted for some 65 years, occurred with the introduction of the circular enamel and painted dial. By 1780 the style shown in drawing I was found alongside more traditional examples. Instead of having a wooden door, only the brass bezel which held the glass opened for winding and setting the hands. This idea persisted throughout the remaining years of craftsman-made cases. The most delicate and pleasing of all circular dial styles, the balloon-shaped case, is illustrated in drawing J. This style of about 1790 is almost always built up in mahogany and pine carcase woods and veneered in satinwood. It was often cross-banded in tulipwood or similar and strung with box and ebony. A shell or oval fan medallion in sand-shaded marquetry usually decorated the lower stages of the front. Cast brass ogee bracket feet complete this most elegant of designs. The topmost stage, forming a support for the finial, was not always included in this design.

Gillows of Lancaster list one of the balloon-shaped cases in their estimate book for 1800 which was made for a 'Mr Bell Lancaster'. This was likely to have been Henry Bell, Watch and Clockmaker, who was known to be working in 1800, but died in 1801. The example shown in Plate 65 was veneered in mahogany and cross-banded in canary wood, with double stringing in 'Black and White'. This was their way of saying ebony and box, which would give a black-and-white effect. Unusually the case is shown with a 'large brass lifting handle' and no medallion in the base, and while costs are shown for parts and labour, no mention is made of the brass bracket feet shown in the drawing:

		£	s	d
A mahogany bracket clock case, crossband mahoy vineard all round the sides, birchin mahoy vinear in the front, banded with canary wood, & a dble string on each side of the band say black & white cross band mahoy O.G. & small hollow, rim, round the glass.				
6 ft 6 of 1 in mahoy in the head, sides and top vineard with mahoy	@ 2s/3d		14	7½
2 ft 6 of ⅜ in mahogany in the back	@ 14d		2	11
4¼ ft of 1 in oak and mahogany birchin vinear in the case & canary wood banding	@ 20d		7	1
Turning—compute				9
Large brass lifting handle				7
Brass lock 6d, one escution 1d. 2½ in brass hinge 4d				11
An ivory knob 2½d, 1 pair small brass but hinges 3d				5½
One brass turnbuckle				3
Glue screws, & incidents			1	6
Making by Simon Bryham 1 week			18	0
Glass for the door, by I Herbert			2	0
Varnishing by Thos Romney			1	6
Setting out the above at large			1	0
		2	11	7

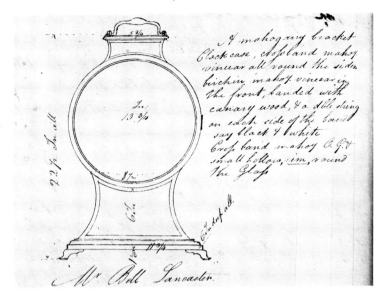

65 A Gillows' sketch for a balloon-shaped bracket clock case of 1800.

Perhaps the last wooden bracket-clock cases made in case-makers' quality and style were those produced in the Regency period. Quality was present in the materials used and, if a trifle heavy in appearance, many of them were very fine. Styles varied from the plain arch-topped case to the quasi-oriental and the woods used were various, including some mahogany but rosewood in veneered form was a firm favourite. Stringing and inlay work was frequently done in brass. Metal mounts were also common, and lion's-mask side handles and pineapple finials were a distinct feature of the time.

Much could be written about the Victorian mantle-clock case, for they were made in wood, porcelain, marble, iron and brass. Many novelty clocks were made and some fantastic styles made as 'show stoppers' around the time of the large international exhibitions of 1851, 1867 and 1889. No particular style existed in the direct line which we have traced back to the mid-17th century. One case does, however, perhaps typify the period more than most: the black Belgian marble clock, which is found in great numbers. These cases had a lasting appeal, for their black architectural cases with incised classical revival decorations and castings conveyed the mood of sorrow felt at the death of Prince Albert, and fitting perfectly with the over-furnished velvet draped interiors of the mid-Victorian period. Although typifying the English middle-class taste these cases were largely made in Belgium and usually imported with a French movement. From this point imported work from many countries caused a decline in the English craft and a general deterioration of standard followed.

Chapter 5

Lantern clocks

Soon as ever the clock struck one I kissed my wife in the kitchen by the fireside, wishing her a merry new yeare, observing that I believe I was the first proper wisher of it this yeare, for I did it as soon as ever the clock struck one.

The Diary of Samuel Pepys.
Entry for the 31st December 1664

The lantern clock, which is the name given to the fully-developed clock of its type, is essentially a weight-driven, brass, wall-mounted striking clock, without wooden case, but generally protected from dust by a back plate of iron and side-doors of brass. It reached its fully-developed and significantly English form in the third quarter of the 17th century, when it incorporated the verge pendulum control. From this date it declined in importance to the mainstream of development in English clock design, although it was produced in country districts well into the 18th century, and as a curious anachronistic Turkish export model as late as 1820.

The immediate precursor of the lantern clock, the somewhat rare (even in its own day) chamber clock of the 16th century, was a larger and more varied type. Chamber clocks were likely to have had foliot balance escapements and possibly were the work of foreign craftsmen in a style similar to German iron wall-clocks of around this time, although their rectangular metal cases were chased and decorated in flowing Renaissance forms. A chamber clock can be seen in various pictures by Hans Holbein at the home of Sir Thomas More, Henry VIII's Chancellor. In common with other chamber clocks and the twelve-hour lantern clocks, More's clock is hung near the ceiling in order to obtain a long period of running before the weights reached the floor.

The lantern clock was the common clock, indeed the only clock, in general use during the early and middle part of the 17th century. Spring clocks were never common or reliable at this early date, although rare table-clocks did exist from the 16th century, such as Nicholas Vallin's drum table-clock. The chamber clock of the 16th century and its natural heir the

66 Marble-cased mantle
clock with French movement
and side ornaments. Clocks
of this type were popular in
England after the death of
Prince Albert. This is a
presentation clock set, and is
dated 1883.

67 Verge lantern clock by Thomas Creed, London, circa 1670. The pendulum, in the shape of an anchor, is placed between the trains. This clock should have decorated side boxes to the doors, and the holes for fixing them can be seen behind the slot in the door.

68 *Left:* Lantern clock by Edward Norris, London, circa 1670. Temple Newsam House, Leeds.

69 *Right:* Lantern clock by Jeremy Spurgin showing the original anchor escapement. The general construction of the clock can be clearly seen.

lantern clock derived their layout from the upright iron bar form of frame used in medieval horology. In this design, wheels and pinions were pivoted into the upright members of the iron frame which were then wedged into position. In the same way brass or iron chamber clocks, and later lantern clocks made with brass posted-frames, all had their pinions supported in three narrow plates. The two outer plates had cruciform arms to support lever work for the strike, and all three were wedged in the top and bottom plates of the main frame. One sometimes hears these clocks referred to as bedpost clocks, probably because the frames resemble a fourposter bed, with its turned feet and top finials. It could even be that these clocks had been hung on the bedpost when used as travelling alarms. However, I think this an unlikely explanation, as they would have been very noisy companions when hung so close to the sleeper. The term lantern clock is most favoured and appears to be the one now accepted for general use, although latten clock (latten is

70 Verge-escapement lantern clock movement, showing the arrangement of trains one behind the other. The dial and going-train on the left, and the striking-train and bob-pendulum can be seen to the right of the picture.

early brass alloy) and Cromwellian clocks are names heard from time to time. There is little wrong with the description Cromwellian clock, for this reflects the time when the clock was at the height of its popularity and manufacture, even though it was also made before and after the Commonwealth period (1649-60). Perhaps an argument against the name Cromwellian is similar to one against calling any flowering floral pattern Jacobean: it is generally used loosely by those who do not know really what they are talking about. I like to think that the lantern clock was so-called because, in its position on the wall, with polished side doors and a rounded bell on top, the clock resembled a simple candle lantern.

Lantern clocks were arranged with their trains one behind the other and the striking work at the back. At first they were driven by two weights, one for each train hung directly from a hook at the end of the rope; the large, somewhat coarsely-pitched nature of their gearing meant that they would only run for twelve hours or so between windings. Control or time-keeping was imposed upon the clock by a balance-wheel es-capement; this was rather insensitive and could be overcome by the pull of the weight if this became too great. The weight was increased or decreased to gain some degree of accuracy, and on some examples a dished top was included on the weight, where lead shot could be added or subtracted, to give a means of adjustment. The balance-wheel at the top of the clock was connected to the vertically-placed verge by a single spoke. As the balance-wheel oscillated to and fro the two pallets shaped like flags on the verge engaged with teeth of the escaping crown-wheel in turn, thus making it necessary to check on the escape-wheel and imposing timekeeping on the clock. The escape-wheel was arranged as the third wheel in the train, and in a vertical plane. Underneath the escape-wheel and protruding from the centre plate, a cock supported the lower pivot of the pallet arbor. Developed from the much earlier foliot balance, the principal governing the action of the balance-wheel was rather like that of swinging a large farmyard gate backwards and forwards: a natural rhythm developed, quicker than which it was impossible to go. A pin was provided to stop the balance-wheel from turning too far in either direction.

Two click springs for pull-winding and two weights were necessary to obtain going and striking in the clock. An additional small weight, and a counter-weight, was also needed to equip the clock with an alarm. These hung down at the back of the clock. The two main lead weights, each about 4 lbs to 5 lbs of lead, hung directly from the rope looped over the spiked pulley in the clock. The going-weight generally fell to the left and the strike-weight to the right. This arrangement meant that the weights would look balanced and not foul each other as they descended. Since the strike-weight fell to the right, and the rope was looped directly to the main pin-wheel, the hammer clearly needed to be situated on the right side of the clock. The hammer was later moved to the other side of the clock, and this became its accepted position in all but the later 30-hour plate-framed long-case clock. A firm indicator in identifying an early balance-wheel lantern clock, even if it has been subsequently altered, is therefore the placing of the hammer to the right of the clock when viewed from the front.

These clocks were about $15\frac{1}{2}''$ high to the top of the bell finial and $5\frac{3}{4}''$ at their widest point. Narrow chapter rings, a single simple hand and stubby finials and feet characterised them. Makers of these early lantern clocks were relatively few in number and all known examples bear the names of a fairly small group of no more than a dozen men all working in London. These included Ahasuerus Fromanteel and his family, in business with a variety of family members at Mosses Alley, Southwark; his son-in-law Thomas Loomes later at the Mermaid in Lothbury; this had previously been the home and workshop of William Selwood, who was another early maker of balance wheel lantern clocks. William Bowyer too made fine clocks at this time, and his clocks were generally shorter and rather stubby in general outline. Thomas Knifton at the Cross Keys in Lothbury too was a balance-wheel lantern clock maker of good reputation. Clocks made by all these makers and others frequently had an alarm mechanism situated out of the way on the iron backplate of the clock. This was a convenient placing as the back of the clock was always clear of the wall while still being sheltered because of its method of hanging. Only very occasionally were these clocks stood on a bracket; they were generally hung by a stout iron hoop riveted into the top plate of the frame, and protruding backward and horizontally. The clock was kept level by a pair of spurs fixed into the back feet or the backplate at its lowest point. Similar in appearance to the escapement of the clock, the alarm work meant that pallets had to be placed on the hammer staff which was oscilllated by the teeth of the crown-wheel when the weight, which was hung from a pulley behind the crown-wheel, was released. The double-headed hammer extended upwards and struck the main bell from inside. The alarm continued to sound until the weight was fully run down. The alarm was set on a special disc, on the top front dial-plate and behind the single hour-hand. When set, the pipe which carried the alarm-disc progressed with the hour-wheel and hand. A pin on this mechanism released the alarm at the appointed hour. The necessary lever work was pivoted from behind the dial-plate and carried through to the backplate of the clock, where the alarm work is situated. A clock which originally had an alarm, subsequently removed, can be identified by the plain, undecorated circular area, consisting of 2″ of the dial surrounding the hand boss, and also the existence of the pivot hole for the alarm arbor pivot above the chapter XI on the dial-plate corner. On pendulum lantern clocks with the hammer placed to the left-hand side of the clock, the alarm arbor could be on the right-hand side and consequently pivoted through the dial-plate. The example shown by Thomas Creed illustrates this (Plate 67).

Two important developments in horological thinking changed the lantern clock. One of them, the introduction of the pendulum control from Holland in 1658, changed the whole course of clockmaking in England. The debate as to who was the first to introduce control of an escapement by a pendulum as applied to the clock, has gone on for centuries. Many have been claimed as its inventor, including Leonardo da Vinci and Galileo Galilei. However, its first successful application, in a design that subsequently spread to general use, was by the Dutch clockmaker Salomon Coster of The Hague, working to the ideas of the physicist Christiaan Huygens of Zulichem in 1657. Huygens published these ideas and others in a work entitled *Horologium* in 1658.

Working with Salomon Coster in Holland was John Fromanteel, the son of the London clockmaker Ahasuerus. John was a young man probably gaining experience in Holland, but it seems unlikely that his father knew nothing of the important developments there. Shortly after John's return to London in May 1658, Ahasuerus Fromanteel was able to advertise rather grandly, and somewhat mysteriously, what we now know to have been the first pendulum clocks in England. This advertisement was placed in the *Mercurius Politicus* of 28th October 1658. I quote the part dealing with clocks.

'There is lately a way found out for making of clocks that go exact and keep equaller time than any now made without this Regulator examined and proved before his Highness the Lord Protector, by such Doctors whose knowledge and learning is without exception and are not subject to alter by change of weather, as others are, and may be made to go a week, or a month, or a year, with once winding up, as well as those that are wound up every day, and keep time as well; and is very excellent for all House clocks that go either with Springs or Waights: And also Steeple Clocks that are most subject to differ by change of weather. Made by Ahasuerus Fromanteel, who made the first that were in England: You may have them at his house on the Bankside in Mosses Alley, Southwark, and at the sign of the Maremaid in Loathbury, near Bartholomew lane end, London'.

From 1658 therefore, clocks made in London and certainly those by the Fromanteels and their associates, had the short bob pendulum and verge escapement referred to by Fromanteel in his advertising.

The other important change, which was also described by Huygens in his *Horologium*, is the system of looping the clock rope or chain around both going- and strike-train pulleys, in such a way that one endless rope or chain could be used. Pull-up winding, made possible by a single click on the strike-train only, did not interrupt the power to the going train while winding. This provided a means of maintaining power while using only one weight of about 7 lbs. (The drawing of a clock in Huygen's book does not have a strike-train, but a separate pulley and click for the specific purpose of winding while maintaining power to the going-train is shown). The diagram on the left shows how this simple system was applied to the English lantern clock and subsequently to 30-hour clocks through to the end of the long-case clock period in about 1850.

In order that the loops of the rope would not hang crossed

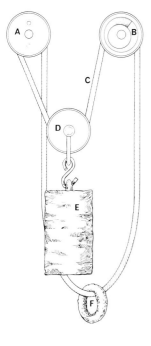

Huygens' endless rope principle for winding and maintaining power:
A Going-side pulley riveted to the first wheel.
B Strike-side pulley with click spring to facilitate winding.
C Endless rope.
D Weight pulley.
E Weight.
F Lead ring to keep rope taut.

and foul each other in action, the weight-pulley suspended in the driving-loop from both going- and strike-trains was hung at the left of the clock. The left side was not chosen arbitrarily. To impart a clockwise motion to the hour-wheel (and hence the hand), the immediate driving member on to which the rope pulley was fixed needs to revolve in anti-clockwise direction, or be pulled downwards from the left. Pairing this action to the action of the strike meant that the strike pin-wheel, also the main drive-wheel, fixed via the winding click to the rope pulley, was also driven to the left. The hammer-placing also needed to be moved to the left so that its tail could be activated by the downward sweep of the hammer-pins to strike the bell from the inside. The incorporation of this endless rope principle coincided with the adoption of finer gearing and larger numbers of wheel teeth. As a result clocks could be made to run for approximately 30 hours at one winding.

The crown-shaped escape-wheel still played a central role after the change from balance-wheel to verge-pendulum. Instead of being the third wheel in the train it now became the fourth, and was moved into a horizontal plane above the top plate of the clock. The third wheel is the contrate wheel, cut with teeth on its flank and so able to transfer the motion to the vertically placed arbor and pinion of the crown-wheel. The 9″-long bob-pendulum was rigidly fastened to the pallet arbor and

71 *Left:* Lantern clock, showing the arrangement of the crown wheel, verge, and bob-pendulum, as well as hoop and spurs for fixing the clock to the wall.

72 *Right:* Travelling alarm by Henry Aske of London, circa 1680, in its original oak carrying box.

made its short, fussy journeys to and fro between the spurs at the back of the clock. The pallet-arbor or verge position just above the crown-wheel is pivoted into a cock behind the front fret and comes backwards across the centre of the crown-wheel; its back support was of a knife-edge design and worked in a V-slot in the back cock. Two flag pallets hang down from the verge. Set at 45°, these intercept the crown-wheel at each swing of the pendulum and impose measured time on the progress of the hand with an accuracy that had never been possible before. The pendulum was placed in precisely the area normally occupied by the alarm work and older balance-wheel clocks which were improved by altering to the new verge pendulum control invariably lost their alarm work as a result. Pendulum lantern clocks, newly-made for those customers needing alarm-work, needed re-thinking and various answers to this problem were devised. Perhaps the most successful idea for the sleepy traveller was to remove the hour strike-train completely and put the alarm work in its place. Unable to strike the hours, the clock was lighter and often much smaller. Some as small as 6″ or 7″ high were made, and some still retain their oak carrying-boxes with partitions and fittings for the secure packing of clock and weights. Lantern clocks of this type are known as bedchamber alarms and were made by the most eminent of makers including Tompion and Knibb. The verge-pendulum escapement was very convenient for travelling clocks or clocks which might be hastily set up. Its design is such that it is not too sensitive and will still go even when not quite level. For this reason these little clocks remained in use well into the second half of the 18th century, long after the normal lantern clock had gone out of vogue for regular domestic use. Very occasionally the sides of the lantern clock were used for mounting an alarm, which meant that the pendulum could be fitted in the conventional rear position. This was not a convenient arrangement as it made side access to the movement difficult. It is frequently necessary to open both side doors of a rope-driven lantern clock and blow out all the dust and fluff which has been accumulated by the action of the rope. If this is not done it picks up on the oil, wraps round pivots and fills the teeth of wheels and pinions. Since the verge-arbor could cross the centre of the crown-wheel at any point the pendulum could be made to work equally well at the side of the clock. This is very rarely seen but is recorded and examples are known. These examples, however, are converted from balance-wheel clocks, and it is my view that this arrangement was to save a backplate-mounted alarm.

A most picturesque and interesting variation enabled the alarm-work to remain on the backplate and the pendulum was moved to the centre of the clock, swinging between the two trains. This simply meant that the strike- and going-arbors were made a little shorter and an additional upright plate was needed in the middle. The space left between the two centre plates, generally about $\frac{3}{4}''$, was ample room in which to swing a pendulum. The novelty value of this arrangement did not pass unnoticed; the conventional idea of a pear-shaped brass bob was replaced by an anchor-shaped elongated bob with flukes protruding out of the case at each side with every swing of the pendulum. Slots were cut into the clock side doors to allow for this and were further elaborated with open-fronted triangular boxes decorated on the top surface by a specially-made brass fret. This greatly increased the width of the clock, and what had begun as a necessary alternative became a decorative feature as well. These winged clocks were extremely popular between 1660 and 1675 and quite a number of them survive. Because of the pendulum side boxes they are known as winged lantern clocks. Even when they have later been converted to the long-pendulum and anchor-escapement, as many were, the clues that tell of the clock's original centre pendulum are unmistakeable unless major alterations to the trains have also been carried out: the existence of four vertical plates instead of three with a $\frac{3}{4}''$ gap between the middle two. The hammer arbor is shortened and pivoted only between the two rear plates so as not to foul the pendulum with its arbor and associated blade-spring. At the left-hand side the lifting arbor, which is needed to trigger off the hour strike, must travel from front to back and so is curved upwards in an inverted 'U' for the same reasons.

The period immediately after 1672 and the introduction of the anchor-escapement and the long-pendulum saw the rapid development and increasing popularity of the long-case clock. Strictly speaking, this rendered the lantern clock out of date. Some were still made however, for the style must have been pleasing to many traditionalists who would consider the long-case to be cumbersome and unnecessary. A lantern clock made at this time by Henry Webster of London (Plate 75) remains unaltered. It was made without an alarm but with an anchor escapement and long pendulum. Another feature of this clock which illustrates a departure from the normal is the mounting of the bell by an internal bell-cage arrangement, while still retaining the traditional top finial with a nut inside the bell for fastening. Towards the end of the 17th century – a period of experiment and innovation – the lantern clock was developed in the hands of a few clever makers to include novel and untypical features. Minute-markings on the chapter-ring and two hands sometimes accompany the use of the long pendulum and in rare cases this was used on verge pendulum clocks. Among others recorded are quarter-chiming clocks, musical clocks incorporating a rotary barrel to activate the hammers, and key-wind lantern clocks with weights suspended on gut-line and running for eight days. Seen in the light of mainstream development these are highly untypical. A clock of this sort offered for sale today should be viewed with suspicion for few were made originally and there will be many others subsequently 'improved'.

Care is necessary in dating a lantern clock, for individual features seen in isolation cannot give a firm indication of its age. Fortunately clues do exist in altered specimens so that detective work, if undertaken carefully, will often reveal all. Spare holes were rarely filled in, for alterations made in years gone by were not done to deceive. Holes in the top plate usually indicate where a cock has been positioned to hold the top pivot of a balance-wheel staff, or of a crown-wheel in the case of a later verge. Similarly holes, usually square, will exist in the centre plate if the bridge, used to bypass the verge

73 *Left:* Verge lantern clock showing the alarm on the iron backplate and a gap between the two trains in which the anchor-shaped pendulum is placed.

74 *Right:* Spring-driven movement with rear-facing winding squares, 'lantern clock hands' and hammer for striking the inside of a bell. This movement was specially made for 'modernising' lantern clocks.

and pivot the vertical crown-wheel, on a balance-wheel clock, has been removed. This bridge may have been retained and altered to accommodate the back-pivot of the contrate-wheel arbor if the clock had been altered to a verge-pendulum after 1658. These old clocks were converted to anchor escapement throughout the 19th century and in this century until very recently. Other features were improved and replaced with very little regard to aesthetic considerations or authenticity. Spring-driven movements were at one time made with fusée arbors extended backwards to provide rear-winding especially for use in 'modernising' lantern clocks. One such, with a pair of 'lantern-clock' hands is illustrated in Plate 74. A balance-wheel lantern clock by William Selwood, which had been converted to anchor-escapement some time ago, is illustrated in Plate 23, on page 39. The anchor is clearly more sophisticated in style than the rest of the clock, but what really gives it away is that it is attached to its arbor not by brazing or by being driven on, but to a collet by two delicate 19th-century screws. Such clues are there if you take the trouble to look. As so often, authentic technical details have been ignored in the interests of 'improving' a fine old clock.

The method of fixing of the large bell in lantern clocks changed little. It was suspended from a bell cage or from straps of four arms radiating from a central point. These were curved round outside the bell and pegged into holes cross-drilled into the very tops of the four corner finials flanking the frets and surmounting the main clock frame. The pegs or pins are a fixture in the ends of the bell-cage arms and are sprung into position. Small pierced, decorative features occur between the arms around the central boss. These are usually more pronounced on examples of London origin and by good makers. Bell-cages are usually made of brass, although iron is used in the case of the Henry Webster clock where the bell-cage fits inside the bell. Very rare indeed, but not unknown, is the bell fixed by a single bell-staff. In all cases the bell is surmounted by a matching finial which gives poise and finish to the clock. In early examples, frets, screwed to the top plate of the frame on three sides of the clock, fill in the awkward area between the top plate and the underside of the bell, and hide the workings of the hammer and the escapement. Frets are a characteristic and highly decorative part of the clock but they can never be regarded as firm indicators of age, particularly when considered in isolation. Some observation can however be made. From the earliest times the base of the front fret, like the central or lower part of the dial plate, occasionally carried

75 Lantern clock by Henry Webster, London, showing the unusual iron bell-cage, which supports the bell from the inside. Temple Newsam House, Leeds.

the maker's name, place of trading, city and so on. When signed in this way on the fret, it must be remembered that frets are only held by two screws and may not be original to the clock. The front fret is always engraved and usually well finished. On better clocks the side frets may also be engraved. Drawing A shows an heraldic fret, so-called because of the central shield. This could be used to record the date of making, maker's initials or even those of the first owner. However, they were often left blank, the maker choosing to sign his work across the fret-base or elsewhere. In this example the supports to the shield are of a foliage design but animals such as unicorns are known. Drawing B shows another early style with a curving design of leaves terminating in blunt-ended scrolls. This design was known to have been used by William Bowyer and William Selwood on their balance-wheel clocks. By far the most common of any design seen is the dolphin fret. Various versions are seen but perhaps the one shown here in drawing C is most typical. This is seen on the very earliest and the very latest lantern clocks and so it must have had an enduring appeal. Drawings A and C are also used in a type, raised up on an arcaded base as shown in drawing D, used here on yet another foliate example. A symmetrical leaf design as shown in drawing E is used occasionally on some London work. This was equally as popular as the dolphin fret with the East Anglian makers of lantern clocks. The next fret, shown in F, shows non-European influence, coming from an out-of-period lantern clock destined for the Turkish market.

Regional versions of the lantern clock were found mainly in

Lantern clock frets:
A Heraldic fret, pre-1650.
B Early fret with blunt-ended scrolls.
C Dolphin fret. The most common type, used throughout the lantern-clock period.
D Foliate fret on an arcaded base. The arcaded section was occasionally applied to all types of frets.
E Fret using a leaf design favoured by some East Anglian clockmakers.
F Fret from a lantern clock for the Turkish market. Islamic features are apparent and include the crescent moon.

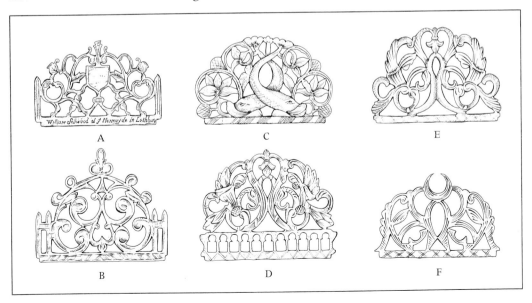

William Selwood at y Mermayde in Lothbury

A   C   E

B   D   F

the south. Since lantern clocks were the first domestic clocks, these regional forms can provide an indication of the areas in which clockmaking began earliest. Isolated examples are sometimes found in an area where a maker was trained in London and then moved to a provincial centre to carry on his work. Thomas Cruttenden of York, by whom a few lantern clocks are known, is an example of this. He had been an apprentice in London but set up a workshop in York after 1679, where he died in 1698. Perhaps it is understandable that no lantern clocks are recorded from far-flung northern areas such as Westmorland and Cumberland, although I am not so sure about Cornwall. A lantern clock or two might be known in an area such as Lancashire with a long clockmaking tradition, but I have seen no mention in any records or books. A number were made in the Midlands however, and in the area which extends towards Bristol in the west. *Somerset Clockmakers* by J. K. Bellchambers illustrates a fine balance-wheel lantern clock by Samuel Stetch of Bristol, and good examples by three other local makers are shown. This suggests quite a colony of makers there in the mid-17th century. William Holloway of Stroud, Gloucestershire, was an early provincial maker of lantern clocks but judging by the appearance of his work and also the Bristol work previously mentioned, there is nothing provincial about the quality.

Most lantern clocks made outside London were made in East Anglia, where the taste for the style lasted well into the 18th century. At this time they were obviously preferred to the oak-cased 30-hour clock, with one or two hands, which was the normal product of many other regions such as Westmoreland, Lancashire, Cheshire and Yorkshire. It is not difficult to see the reason for this preference of the lantern clock: East Anglia is the nearest part of the British Isles to Holland, and many Dutch merchants and craftsmen had settled in East Anglia during the 16th and 17th century. Ahaseurus Fromanteel himself, the London clockmaker, was born in Norwich in 1607 of a Dutch emigré family. His father was a wood-turner, probably employed in the furniture trade. Many ideas which helped develop the English clockmaking industry had come from Holland and a clock in the shape of a lantern which had grown up along with these developments was naturally one which would be revered for many years. The frequency of brick-built Flemish gables in the architecture of this region can be attributed to the import of ideas by Flemish workmen in the same way. The manner of putting brick together in a certain way is still known as Flemish Bond. Even in East Anglia,

76 Early 18th-century long case made to house a lantern clock.

however, the production of clocks did not get underway as early as it did in London and most East Anglian lantern clocks were made after 1700. Some, though, were made in the second half of the 17th century and original verge-pendulum lantern clocks by a number of makers have been recorded. East Anglian lantern clock is a phrase used to describe that group of clocks from the area originally made using the anchor escapement and long pendulum. These clocks were generally typified by their broader chapter-rings and absence of alarm work; otherwise their general appearance and size is very much the same as others from a different time and area. Later in the period the broader chapter-ring occasionally became quite wide in relation to the frame and these clocks, and the provincial travelling-alarms with untypical square dials, with arched tops, became known as sheeps' heads.

In discussing the sheeps' head lantern clock, later travelling-alarms and others, we come to the group of lantern clocks that were clearly made unusually late. Obviously the travelling-alarm might be kept in its box for many years and used only infrequently. Those ordered and newly-made in the late 18th century were still probably the best thing for the job and, unlike the owner of the very first balance-wheel lantern clock, the 18th-century owners of these small portable clocks would be likely also to have a grand long-case clock and maybe a bracket clock for use at home. The fact that small lantern-shaped alarms retained the verge escapement and short bob pendulum provides a clue to its continued popularity. Setting up the clock, perhaps hurriedly, on a makeshift nail in the bedroom of an inn required a stable temperament in the clock if it was to be reliable. The crown-wheel escapement was and still is the least sensitive pendulum escapement, and will go reliably when not absolutely level.

By far the most interesting group of lantern clocks of the ones that persisted 'out of period' are those made for the Turkish market. The Muslim Ottomans had a delight in English clocks and watches and they imported them in great numbers over a long period of time. The brassy lantern clock was a firm favourite and, perhaps because it came nearest to their ideal, they caused it to be made until the early 19th century.

The crescent was a favourite Turkish symbol, and suggests the Islamic religious preoccupation with the moon. We have previously seen this depicted on the drawing of the typical Turkish-market fret on page 99 (F). The photograph of the clock by Isaac Rogers clearly illustrates this influence in the engraving of its side doors (a very untypical practice for

77 Lantern clock made for the Turkish market by Isaac Rogers of London. Islamic features may be seen in the numerals, frets and the side door.

England). Isaac Rogers was Master of the Clockmakers' Company in 1813 and we may assume that it could be as late or even later than this.

Although this book divides styles and types of clocks into separate chapters, the reality is never as clearly defined as that. Some lantern clocks which had originally been given a square arched-dial and a wooden hood became hanging wall-clocks. This type of clock was seen, albeit rarely, in non-lantern clock areas during the early 18th century. These are not to be confused with the more sophisticated hanging wall-clocks which had plate frames, key-wound movements and were made in the early long-case clock period; these can be

78 Small hooded alarm with posted movement by James Field, Dunstable; after 1758.

described as identical in most respects to the long-cased clock but without a trunk.

Sometimes a lantern clock was cased up in a country-style long-case of oak or pine. It is likely that some were made up in this way during the early 18th century but it equally seems possible that some customers chose the case when the clock was new. It is obvious that the cases are made specially for lantern clocks as their upright elongated hood-doors are sometimes arch-topped and showing the top fret and sometimes square-cut when the front fret of the clock has been removed. Their simple style and manner of construction usually underlines their age and purpose.

Chapter 6

Long-case clocks

1724 July 10th Bought at Derby Market from Wolley of Codnor, square oak clock Paid £4. 10s. 00d. He wanted £5.

From the diary of a Lincolnshire farmer

Long wooden cases were used to house certain lantern clocks fairly late on in the lantern-clock period. However, this is not a real pointer to the development of the long case, as it took place. Lantern clocks cased in this way were not usual until the early 18th century and the first true long-case clocks in England were made, in quite a different way, soon after the introduction of the pendulum in 1658. From the clocks which survive and the evidence we have already discussed about the pendulum, it would seem likely that Ahasuerus Fromanteel was the first to make long-case clocks in Britain.

A new method of winding the clock was devised at the very outset of long-case clock manufacture. It would be too easy to forget to pull up a weight hidden behind a closed door and the clock would stop, possibly causing great disruption in the household. It was no easy matter in those days to set the clock to time, for reference had to be made to the sundial, and its reading converted to equal time as shown on the clock dial, by referring to tables specially provided for this purpose. It was understood that running a clock with rope was a crude and dusty business. The spikes in the clock pulleys shredded the rope and quickly made it unserviceable. Chains too had their disadvantages. If a chain twists slightly and the link does not quite fit over the spike in the movement pulley, then a sudden judder is likely to occur in the clock. Greater time between windings and smoother running could be achieved by using thinner lines and winding them many times round a grooved drum or barrel. This drum was mounted on the same arbor as the main wheel in each train. When provided with a click-and-ratchet arrangement, which freed the barrel in one direction, the clock could be wound by key. This was easily arranged by making the front of the barrel-arbor terminate in a winding square on to which a cranked key could be placed through a

79 Early architectural long-case clock by Fromanteel, London. British Museum, London.

hole in the dial. Until this date it had been customary to place the strike-train behind the going- or watch-train in the movement, but now this was no longer convenient if key winding and greater duration was to be achieved. A change came about in the layout of the clock movement which was both fundamental and very simple. It provided many advantages and facilitated the rapid development of clockmaking skills towards the many refinements and innovationary features which followed.

The plate movement was made up of almost exactly the same units as the lantern type of movement, in different proportion. Instead of the brass plates being used top and bottom as in the lantern clock, they were now arranged back and front and held together by somewhat shorter pillars at each corner. The wheel arbors could now be pivoted directly into these plates with trains side-by-side, giving front access for winding at any point convenient to the clockmaker. Decorative finials and the brass feet were left out of this arrangement. Usually the plate-pillars were riveted into the backplate and protruded only a little way through in order to be secured with pins or latches. The movement stood firmly on the lower edges of the upright plates. More complicated movements, involving the use of heavy weights, had more than the usual four pillars in their movement construction; five or six pillars were common in these examples. Later London-made examples, and some of the best country work, used five pillars as the normal arrangement. The extra pillar comes between the two winding barrels, giving extra support and stopping the plates from flexing where the stress is greatest.

Pillars in the 17th century were seen by makers as an area for decorative turning. Different workshops showed characteristic variations in this treatment. Baluster shapes were usual and these are either symmetrically turned to give equal weight to both ends or, less frequently turned to emphasise the part nearer the backplate. Towards the year 1700, however, these too took on a more general character and most work done in London and the provinces at this time had delicately turned and finned pillars as shown by Plates 81 and 92.

The development of the long pendulum and the associated anchor-escapement allowed great strides to be made towards the good timekeeping which still typifies long-case clocks. They were first recorded as used, not on a domestic clock, but on a tower clock made for a Cambridge College, by William Clements about 1672. This clock can now be seen in the Science Museum, London. There is still debate as to who invented the anchor escapement; some authorities credit it to William Clements himself. What is certain is that there was much experimentation, discussion and correspondence in the late 1660s between people interested in horological development. Dr. Robert Hooke, the eminent physicist and member of the newly-formed Royal Society, was at the centre of these developments and caused Thomas Tompion to make him clocks with experimental anchor escapements of the long-pendulum type. At one stage, when he was impatiently awaiting the making of a clock to test one of his theories, he flew into a rage and 'Fel out with Thompian' calling him 'a clownish churlish Dog'. During his work on escapements, Hooke demonstrated to the Royal Society a small watch controlled by a very long pendulum. Hooke claimed to have invented the anchor-escapement in 1665 but although this is quite possible, no proof exists to substantiate the claim. John Flamsteed, the first Astronomer Royal, also joined in the development of the anchor escapement and Tompion made two precision clocks using the anchor-escapement and long pendulum which were set up in the new Royal Observatory at Greenwich for Flamsteed's use in experiments on the equation of time. Letters exist from Flamsteed to Richard Towneley of Towneley Hall, near Burnley, Lancs, explaining the intricacies of the new

80 *Left:* Eight-day long-case movement seen from below. Three of the five plate pillars can be seen. Holes in the two outer pillars are for screws fixing the clock to the seatboard.

81 *Right:* Finned pillars typical of London and good provincial work at this time. The clock movement is by John Williamson of Leeds, circa 1690.

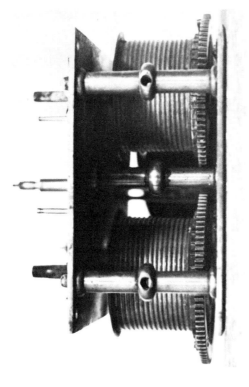

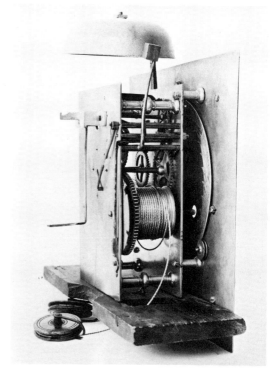

escapement and Towneley, himself a scientist and experimenter in horological matters, also made suggestions for its refinement. People tried pendulums as long as 61", almost reaching the bottom of the case for a brief period, as was previously mentioned in the chapter on cases. Eventually the seconds pendulum, which was some 39" long, was found to be most convenient and this, coupled with an anchor-recoil escapement, was used subsequently on almost all long-case clocks made for household use. Another advantage of the seconds pendulum was that the escape-arbor extended forwards and, when provided with a hand, gave a seconds indicator to the clock. The pendulum was so central to thinking in clockmaking circles at this time that the word 'pendulum' was often used in place of the word 'clock'. I am not sure whether it was because of its regal dominance over the motions of the clock or to honour King Charles II, but the seconds pendulum came to be known as the Royal Pendulum.

Equipped with these developments and their undoubted skills, the best clockmakers in London developed the craft to an exceptionally high standard and the period from about 1670 to 1700 became known as the golden period of English clockmaking. Long-case clocks were made to go for a month, three months, or even a year at one winding. In fact year-clocks were more common at this period than ever since. The addition of extra wheels to the train made year-clocks possible, but the weights needed to keep the clock going and to strike for a year were very heavy indeed. An eight-day clock, intended for weekly winding with a day in reserve in case you forgot, had four wheels in its going-train and generally needed a weight of between 10 lbs and 16 lbs to drive it. The strike-train was geared in a similar way and used a similar weight. A month-going clock usually had five wheels in its train and weights of about 24 lbs each. There were various ways in which a maker might 'gear up' a year-clock, but one way was by using six wheels and a vast differential of gearing and pitch between the main wheel which bore the winding-barrel and weight, and the escape-wheel. The main-wheel was massively constructed whilst the escape-wheel was more delicately made than even the ones on the eight-day clock. The weight needed to drive such a train would be in the region of 50 lbs. Some year-clocks are timepieces only, as the amount of weight needed for a striking-train as well was excessive indeed. During a year some 60,000 blows would be struck on the bell to record every hour. Joseph Knibb invented a method of striking which reduced this considerably and, because it related to the hours engraved

Below: A posted-frame construction as used in lantern clocks. *Bottom:* A plate-frame movement in which trains were placed side by side.

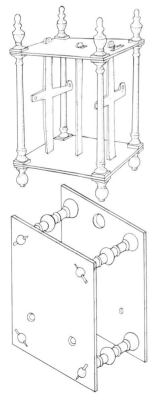

82 A 12″ square dial of an eight-day clock by Henry Hindley of Wigan.

on the chapter-ring, it was known as Roman-striking. Two bells and two hammers were provided in the movement, a blow on the deep bell indicating the Roman figure V and a blow on the lighter bell the figure I; X was indicated by two blows on the deeper bell. Thus XII would sound with two blows on the deep bell and two blows on the light bell—a saving of eight blows. Though this was a good idea it did not last and its use was restricted largely to Knibb himself.

The application of a long pendulum, an improved escapement and the constant force of a lead weight, gave such good timekeeping results, that the difference between meantime (the division of a day into 24 equal hours as shown by the clock) and solar time (as measured from the motions of the sun) became very obvious. The difference at its extreme periods is $16\frac{1}{2}$ minutes fast on 4th November and $14\frac{1}{2}$ minutes slow on 12 February. Since clocks at this period could be accurate to within one minute per week, great frustrations would be experienced in trying to set them to time with a sundial alone. Only on four days a year does equal time and solar time coincide exactly. Many makers were aware of this problem and issued a printed table of the differences enabling the sundial reading to be modified to equal time. Other makers made ingenious clocks which showed solar and equal time on separate rings. Often these were highly involved and consisted of full-sized chapter-rings side by side, worked by two movements in the same large case. Daniel Quare made a clock of this type in about 1710. Joseph Williamson made a clock with a dial at each side of the clock and placed back-to-back each side

83 The Morgan Lowry year clock, showing the massive weights for going- and strike-trains. The key is in place on the winding square of the going-train. Abbey House Museum, Kirkstall, Leeds.

84 Winding key of the Morgan Lowry year clock (Plate 83; left) showing its long cranked handle for winding the huge weights. A more conventional eight-day clock key is shown to the right. Abbey House Museum, Kirkstall, Leeds.

of a common, but complicated, movement. One dial showed equal time and the other meantime. However, these were very rare and special clocks. They were never intended to be used in a domestic situation, but were made as showpieces and found in palaces and country houses where they were no doubt a good advertisement and a talking-point for all who saw them. Less flamboyant equation-clocks doubtless did have a scientific use in observatories and some fine ones of this type were made by Thomas Tompion using the more conventional long-case form without any exaggerated variations. Some high-quality clocks became so accurate that even the amount of time it took to wind the weight was thought to be important. Ingenious makers took this into consideration and devised a system of maintaining power for key-wound clocks. The most usual method employed at the end of the 17th century involved the use of discs or shutters held in place behind the winding-holes by a strong blade-spring. Pulling these aside by a cord or lever to place a key on the winding-square also lifted a bolt or lever into engagement with a wheel in the going-train. This exerted enough pressure on the wheel to keep the train in motion during the few moments of winding. Restoration of power and the advance of the wheel gradually dislodged the bolt, allowing it to return to its normal position. The shutters sprang back into position at the same time. The clock shown here by Hindley de Wigan (Plate 82) has this feature, and the little catch which pushes the shutters aside can just be seen above the mouth of the face of the spandrel decoration in the bottom-right.

Strike-work in clocks was also changed and improved. Clockmakers put most of their energies into developing the escapement, and changes in strike-work came slightly later. The rack-and-snail method of striking was introduced by the avant-garde makers in 1675-80. To explain the advantages of this method over the previous count-wheel strike which had been used since medieval times, it is first necessary to explain how the older method worked. Like the going-train, the strike-train, is made up of a number of wheels and pinions: three wheels in the lantern and 30-hour long-case clocks and four in the more usual eight-day clock. Three main factors have to be considered in order that the train can perform its basic function of reliably recording the passing hours on a bell (bells were always used on traditional English clocks until the 19th century). A wheel low down in the train needs to be pinned in order to pick up, or push aside, the tail of the hammer. As the hammer falls off the revolving pins, a blade-spring, also

bearing on the hammer-arbor, causes the hammer to make a swift light blow to the bell. The speed of the train is also important if an even, measured rhythm is to be given to the strike. A hurried and erratically struck bell would be very unpleasant to hear and, if the train ran too quickly, locking-up at the end of the strike would be a hazardous business causing rapid wear and even breakage. To give this even strike and smooth locking an additional feature is put into the bell train. Made in the shape of a flat rotating vane, it is known as the fly. It is made with a friction fit to its arbor. The fly's resistance to the air slows down the train and its friction fit allows it to travel on briefly after the hours have been struck and absorb the power of the train and give smooth locking. The train is unlocked by the lifting-piece, positioned by the motion work between the dial and the front plate of the clock. This is raised by a pin on the motion work itself about five minutes before the hour; the pin unlocks the strike work by lifting the locking detent from the locking pin or slot, and allows it to proceed a short way before being held temporarily by a pin especially placed to catch the warning-piece. When the hour is reached, the lifting-piece falls from the lifting-pin and in turn allows the warning-piece to fall and set the strike train in motion. These features are common to all striking methods and it is the way in which the hours are counted that is different and gives the two main types of strike train their names.

85 *Left:* Posted-frame movement of a clock by John Ismay of Oulton, Cumberland. The count-wheel for the strike can be seen to the left of the picture.

86 *Right:* Rack-striking, plate-framed 30-hour clock by Thomas Lister, Halifax, circa 1760.

The first method was known as count-wheel strike and consisted of a brass count-wheel or disc, slotted irregularly around the circumference. The distance between the slots represented the duration of strike and the lever (or detent) which falls into the slots causes the locking at the end of the strike; thus the area for twelve blows is the greatest and the distances get progressively shorter towards the lower numbers. There is no distance at all for striking one and the detent falls back into the same slot. Usually count-wheels revolved every twelve hours and their layout was based on 78 divisions – the number of blows struck by the clock in that period. This is clearly visible in the left of Plate 85 which I hope will clarify this rather complicated explanation. The wrong name of locking-plate strike is sometimes used when describing this method. This suggests that the progression of the strike-train is halted by the detent holding in the count-wheel slots. This is not so. A separate wheel on which is mounted a stop-pin or a slotted-hoop is provided for the actual locking-up. The detent which drops into the count-wheel slots is directly connected to a further detent which falls against this stop at the appropriate time. The count-wheel is, as its correct name implies, a device for counting or measuring the blows.

On lantern clocks and during the verge-pendulum period of long-case clocks, the count-wheel was mounted externally at the back of the movement. Later it was situated within the plates and usually mounted on the side of the strike main-wheel, which also makes one revolution every twelve hours. At first it was mounted behind the wheel nearest the backplate but later it was moved and placed between the wheel and the winding barrel.

The count-wheel system can easily get out of step with the clock. Care has to be taken, when setting the hands, to let each hour strike out, as it is passed. Once out of step the clock has to be struck round to the correct hour by lifting the detent out of the count-wheel until the correct hour is reached. When very worn, as many old clocks are today, this mechanism is prone to get out of step. A common problem is that it will fail to lock-up after a strike, running two or more numbers into one and getting the sequence mixed up. Even when well-adjusted this system had its disadvantages and one of them was that it could not be made to repeat the hours struck; once past the count-wheel could only measure the next hour. In the days of the candle, before the invention of the safety match, obtaining an instant light to check the time at night would have been very inconvenient, and a strike-repeating clock was obviously useful. This feature was used principally in portable clocks, but more long-case clocks than are generally realised were also equipped with repeating facilities. This was particularly true for clocks made in provincial centres after about 1750. Passing the clock in an unlit hall, one only had to pull the repeat cord to make the clock sound the last hour. The newly developed rack-strike could repeat naturally if provided with a simple blade-spring and cord extending from the strike lifting-piece to the outside of the case. The snail – which is the part that determines the number of blows struck – is principally connected to the hour-wheel of the motion work and so is advanced at the same time as the hands. In this way the strike cannot get out of step and when in good repair it monitors accurately the hours shown on the dial, however many times the repeat may be used. There is a further advantage, in that if a fault arises in the striking of one particular hour it does not necessarily throw the whole sequence out of step, and the hands can be set without waiting for the hours to strike out, although it is advisable to allow the twelve to do so for fear of breaking the rack-tail. The reason for this can be seen in the drawing on this page. The rack-strike technique was more reliable but more expensive to make. Using the same methods of unlocking, warning and lifting of the hammer-tail as the count-strike did, the difference was in the way that the hours were counted. The diagram shows the front of a rack-strike movement as it would appear with the dial removed.

The count-wheel strike continued in use, even on some quite sophisticated eight-day clocks made in London well into the 18th century. Country makers, particularly in the Lancashire region, favoured this type of strike for their eight-day clocks through into the 19th century; and the 30-hour long-case clock, whether made in birdcage or in plate form, used it almost exclusively. The count-wheel was rear-mounted in both cases. Just occasionally a plate-framed 30-hour clock will be found with a rack-strike, but this is highly untypical and quite rare. Plate 86 shows the movement of one such clock made about 1760 by Thomas Lister of Halifax.

·Refinements of the anchor-escapement were discussed and experimented with almost immediately after its introduction. The first anchor was so-called because it resembled the downturned flukes of a ships anchor. The shape of the teeth of the escape-wheel gave a recoil action to the train, causing it to halt and make a momentary backward gesture before dropping forward on to the opposite pallet. This can be seen if you look at the seconds hand of a normal eight-day long-case clock. It

Diagram showing the working parts of a rack-striking eight-day clock as it would appear with the dial removed. The snail (A) can be seen attached to the hour-pipe, immediately in front of the hour-wheel. The snail revolves with the hour hand; the highest point on its circumference represents one o'clock and the lowest twelve o'clock. The rack (B) has teeth set on its top surface, each one representing a single blow on the bell. A pin on the tail of the rack (C) drops against the snail's edge just before the hour. The whole of this unit is mounted on a pin (D), and the spring (E) helps to throw the rack-tail on to the surface of the snail. Shortly before the hour the warning lever (F) falls from a lifting pin on wheel (G) to free the train and allow the rack to be gathered up by a small gathering pallet (H). The number of teeth gathered (and consequently the number of blows struck on the bell) depends on the distance the rack tail falls to the surface of the snail. While gathering is taking place the rack is prevented from falling back by the rack hook (I). At the end of the strike the train is usually locked by the extension at the side of the gathering-pallet engaging with a pin on the left side of the rack-top (J). A repeat-cord, when fitted, was usually fastened to the point (K) on the lifting piece; when pulled, it caused the clock to repeat its last strike.

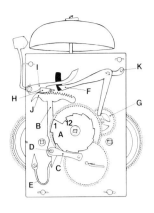

may seem a strange arrangement but it was partly the shape of the teeth of the wheel, and the pallets, which caused this recoil that gave impulse to the pendulum to keep it going. As early as 1675 Tompion developed a style of escapement which was described as dead-beat, because of its precise and accurate action involving no recoil and consequent better timekeeping qualities. But the credit for inventing a true dead-beat escapement is given to Tompion's newphew-in-law and successor George Graham. Graham had been born in Cumberland and travelled to London as a boy. He became an apprentice to Henry Aske, and trained to be a clockmaker for seven years. On the completion of his training he joined Tompion as a journeyman and was possibly responsible for many clocks made in Tompion's name. Precision timekeeping was Graham's special interest and he must have had ample opportunity to see all the latest developments as they occurred in Tompion's workshop. A proven dead-beat escapement whose pallets caused no recoil but worked with a positive sliding action was made by him about 1720, and its principal uses were for observatory and fine regulator clocks, where timekeeping with a high degree of accuracy was essential. His clocks were so accurate that a normal pendulum hung on a simple iron rod was not considered good enough for precise timekeeping because the rod varied with changes of temperature. Graham was a great believer in the use of mercury in his work. As well as making many fine mercury barometers he adopted its properties of expanding when warmed to make a mercurially-compensated pendulum. This worked very well. He described it to the Royal Society, of which he was a very active member, and made examples for his dead-beat regulators in the early 1720s. The length of a pendulum (from the point of suspension to the centre of oscillation, generally considered to be the centre of the pendulum bob) regulates the speed at which it swings. The iron rod of a pendulum naturally expands when warmed and contracts when cooled, sufficiently for the seasons to upset the timekeeping of a fine clock. A glass jar partially filled with mercury was suspended in a stirrup at the base of an iron pendulum and expanded upwards on warming, thus counteracting the downward expansion of the iron rod. This principle was highly successful in its day and was used for many years in precision clocks.

John Harrison, best-known for his work on the marine chronometer, also developed a complicated pendulum which was highly regarded and used more regularly on precise clocks than any other. Harrison too developed his pendulum in the

87 Compensated pendulum of the type by John Ellicot made up of brass and iron components acting on hinged levers, in a fine regulator by John Grant. The Worshipful Company of Clockmakers, Guildhall, London.

1720s, working in Lincolnshire before coming to London in order to promote his life's work on the marine chronometer. His pendulum was known as the grid-iron pendulum and was constructed of nine rods, some of brass, some of iron. The differing expansion rates of the two metals and the way in which they were held together to suspend the heavy brass bob gave extremely good results in timekeeping throughout the seasons.

After the mid-18th century London makers did not make as many long-case clocks as before. Nevertheless the quality of the ones that were made was extremely high. Cases of mahogany were made on simple lines but movements were of the highest order and, with some exceptions in clocks for the domestic market, this was the time of the precision-regulator long-case clock. The precision-regulator almost certainly incorporated a dead-beat escapement, one of the temperature-compensated pendulums mentioned, and some kind of maintaining power for use while winding. A month duration was thought to be a good period of going for regulator clocks although, in common with domestic clocks, eight days was most common. Dial layout could be unconventional to do away with extra motion work which was detrimental to timekeeping properties. Hours might be shown through a lunette aperture in the centre of the dial. Seconds were normally shown, while minutes would be shown around a minute ring in conventional plan. Strike-work and other indications were absent in a true regulator-clock. John Ellicot, Thomas Mudge and William Dutton were all highly skilled makers of clocks of this type. John Ellicot, who worked at a slightly later date than Graham and Harrison, designed his own compensated pendulum. It looks less complicated than the other two described but it used the differing expansion rates of brass and iron just as Harrison's grid iron does. Ellicot's pendulum is known as a compensated pendulum. There was a fourth way in which the expansion rate of a pendulum could be minimised and this method was cheap enough to make it popular for some types of long-case pendulum clocks during the late-18th century. This was to use a piece of wood to make the pendulum rod. While not perfect this gave a far more stable rate than the ordinary iron rod.

London clockmakers in the early long-case clock period devoted their energies to making the clock go for a longer duration than had previously been possible, and very few 30-hour long-case clocks were made. Even so, some are known, including top makers. These generally had the conventional posted movement, count-wheel strike and of course retained the pull-wind. Provincial makers had not yet begun production of the 30-hour clock on a large scale. At this time they were divided into two groups, those who had London connections or training, and made quite sophisticated eight-day or even the odd month-clock in the London tradition, and a much smaller body of makers working in country places who made unsophisticated pull-wind clocks based on lantern form and copied from clocks they had seen by other more capable makers. This was more common in the south of England for in the north before 1720 very few 30-hour clocks of any type are known. Traditional lantern-clock areas can therefore be considered to be leaders in 30-hour clockmaking. Care is needed, however, in defining the age of a long-case clock with birdcage or posted frame construction. This need not necessarily be an early design. Some makers from traditional areas used the arrangement on all their 30-hour clocks until the end of the brass-dial clock period and white-dial clocks featuring this type of movement are sometimes seen. Simplification of the framework of the movement is a pointer in identifying clocks made after this first quarter of the 18th century. The pleasing turned posts gave way to plain iron strips riveted into both top and bottom plates of the movement and on some the plates too are made from thin iron sheet. The reverse may equally apply, and brass could have been used throughout for either material that came easiest to hand would be used, but of course in either case brass was still used for the upright strips into which the arbors were pivoted. The posted movement on the country 30-hour clocks was generally used in traditional lantern-clock areas, but exceptions are found from time to time and so should be borne in mind when identifying a discovery. Plate 85 shows a posted movement and a large square dial of a clock by John Ismay of Oulton, near Wigton in Cumberland. It seems unlikely that this clock would have been made after 1720, but this is an early date and the clock has an unusually large dial for that time. Unfortunately the original case does not exist, but it must have been a fairly simple oak example, compatible with the crude but pleasing style of this movement. I know of one other posted-framed movement and square brass-dialled clock made in a non-traditional area, by Anthony Demaine of Skipton, Yorkshire. This is a clock with two hands, dating from 1770 and housed in its original pine case.

A country maker may often have asked his customers whether they wanted one hand or two, when ordering a 30-hour long-case clock. It could be argued that the persistence of the style of using only one hand on such a clock along with the posted-frame movement was just another lingering lantern-clock feature. Its use was, however, just as common on plate-framed clocks made in various areas until the middle of the 18th century. While 30-hour clocks with one hand only do not form a massive proportion of the total output, there were many made. This tells us that they were a distinct favourite in some country districts. The simplicity would also help to keep down the cost of making the clock and this is probably why, of the few anonymous clocks which exist, a good portion of these are single-handed. Unfortunately many of these humble creations have been altered over the years and given a different movement, usually an eight-day one with two hands. Drilling of the dial-plate to gain access to the winding squares frequently spoilt the engraving on the dial plate centre or even fouled the edge of the chapter-ring on smaller examples. A chapter-ring engraved with divisions for quarter-hours only and no minute-circle clearly gives away this alteration. Often the two substituted hands were of an unsuitable type and too large for the dial. matching brass hands made for larger white dials were commonly used for these 'improvements'. We may feel shocked that these acts of vandalism took place at all, but even 70 years ago a clock was only considered a machine for telling

88 Country long-case 30-hour clock with one hand by Elizabeth Hunt, Overton, near Basingstoke; mid-18th century.

the time, and it would be cheaper to modernise than to replace. Even so it is harder to accept that this sort of thing went on, than it is to accept an escapement modernisation which at least did not spoil the appearance of the dial. Still more difficult to accept is that these and similar alterations are carried out today by people who should know better. Only last year I was approached by a very reputable gentleman in the antique trade who wanted to substitute an eight-day movement for a 30-hour one in a long-case clock. The reason was that his customers did not like winding their clocks every day. It seems however that they don't mind their old clocks being butchered and consequently reduced in interest and value.

So far I have talked a great deal about the nature and make-up of posted movements and not so much about the variations that can be seen in the plate-movement from different work-shops. While the movement of the eight-day clock tended to be a fairly conservative area with no more recent innovation than the rack-strike of 1675, the country-made 30-hour clock tended to be more of an individual product, displaying un-expected and odd features from differing workshops up and down the country. Odd ways of doing things enable us to identify a maker by his movement alone. Generally plates were oblong, slightly taller than wide and held by a pillar at each corner. Thomas Ogden of Halifax almost always made his clock plates with a shallow arched top, while Christopher Johnson of Knaresborough frequently cut away a large semi-circular area at the base of his plates, leaving the appearance of plates with French feet. Perhaps the most curious plates can be seen on 30-hour clocks made by Will Snow of Padside, Yorkshire, for his were completely skeletonised in the interests of economy. The last two makers mentioned also incorporated the escapement-arbor between the plates with a riveted-in steel back-cock for pendulum suspension only. In Will Snow's movements steel was also used for the pillars and these were made parallel and completely undecorated. The customer who could only afford a 30-hour clock and as a result felt some shame in having it in his house, was catered for with a little deceit. Dummy winding-squares were put behind an eight-day type of dial to give the appearance of a key-wound clock. This was done on both brass- and white-dial examples in the 18th century. To com-plete the illusion, a seconds indicator was sometimes provided, even if it meant putting an idler wheel into the movement to reverse the direction of the escape wheel, for on a normal 30-hour, three-wheel train the escape-wheel runs in an anti-clockwise direction. Various methods of fitting dummy squares were adopted but generally they were simply screwed into the front plate of the clock or fixed behind the dial holes on a sheet-metal bridge. On some white-dial examples the deception was really cheapened for the squares were merely painted on to the surface of the dial—a decoration that would fool nobody.

Ninety-nine per cent of all 30-hour clocks have count-wheel strike. Very few have rack-and-snail striking because in some ways it defeats the object of making a cheaper clock. However, it did add to the reliability of the strike-work and give a repeating facility if this was desired, while still not reaching the cost of making an eight-day clock. One such is illustrated by Thomas Lister of Halifax (Plate 86) and is a good example of work by this fine provincial maker. A very odd variation in strike-work is that used by Sam Deacon of Barton in the movement of a square-drilled 30-hour clock dated December 1773 and numbered 44. The count-wheel is unconventionally placed inside the movement and pivoted over the main wheel-arbor towards the backplate. The outer rim of this wheel is not slotted but toothed like a normal wheel. The wheel is advanced by a pin mounted in the second wheel of the train which engages these teeth. This doubles as the warning- and locking-wheel. Counting the strike is done by pins along the front side of the

90 Plain posted frame movement with anchor escapement and count-wheel strike by Jeremy Spurgin.

count-wheel and the detent is lifted by these pins to cause the locking. A simple hammer blade-spring is screwed to the bottom-right pillar and the pillars themselves are completely parallel except for the enlarged area at each end. These oddities, along with other unexpected and charming features, make the collecting of country 30-hour clocks an area which still has exciting possibilities.

After the middle of the 18th century provincial clockmaking really got under way and most towns and some villages could boast a clockmaker in the community. Some towns had many clockmakers, which probably indicates the increasing market for clocks at this time. Yorkshire and Lancashire makers thrived particularly well and considering the number of clocks made and the undoubted quality of many of them, they can almost be said to have taken over where London makers left off. To qualify this statement, the changes tended to be merely stylistic, for the movement continued to be made in plate form with anchor-recoil escapement and rack-strike on eight-day clocks with little variation until the end of the long-case period. Things were not, however, as dull as this may sound. Individual makers had methods of making even the most everyday features exciting and fresh. Screw heads were sometimes shaped to look like serpents, tails of springs and other steel parts were delicately chamfered and filed, and in the days before the Birmingham movement, the front plate was nearly always interestingly scribed for the layout of the trains.

In provincial work, fancy striking is extremely rare. The usual form of strike expected in a long-case clock was for hour-striking only on a bell. The Dutch fashion of sounding the half-hours on a smaller bell never caught on in England. Similarly I have only seen, or heard of, ting-tang quarters or elaborate quarter-chiming on early London clocks. Musical long-case clocks exist and the idea of adding a third train to play music appealed to a number of makers throughout the country. These usually occur in the second half of the 18th century and most seem to be from the period of the final phase of the brass dial clock. Like a musical box, the musical train of a clock makes use of a revolving barrel, which is often pinned for a number of tunes. The pins push against and activate the hammers when the train is set in motion and the music is played on a nest of bells. The usual number in the nest is eight bells which form a complete scale. Arranged in order of size, these are usually fixed to a common staff, spaced by leather washers, and look like a stack of saucers on their sides. The number of hammers vary. Some bells may be struck by two hammers and the least-used bells by only one. Barrels which are pinned for more than one tune are made to slide horizontally so that a different set of pins are in line with the hammer tails. Tunes can usually be selected manually by moving a pointer set against a ring on the dial. The titles of the tunes are often engraved round this ring and very occasionally the clock may have a built-in facility to select a tune for each day. Some years ago I made notes about a musical clock that passed through my workshop, by John Hall of Beverley circa 1785. This clock played four tunes, and a Psalm for Sundays, on eight bells, struck by thirteen hammers. Tunes could be set manually but the clock was made to do this automatically by an arrangement of levers and stepped cams. Days and tunes are engraved round the selector ring:

Sunday – Psalm 149
Monday – Britain Strike Home
Tuesday – Lady Coventry's Minuet
Wednesday – Foot's Minuet
Thursday – Britain Strike Home
Friday – Lady Coventry's Minuet
Saturday – Foot's Minuet

The tune was played and then the hour followed, struck on the hour-bell.

The general arrangement of trains, which relates to most clocks of this type, is to have the hour strike-train on the left, the going-train in the centre of the movement and the musical-train on the right. The Hall clock which was made in this way has many features including a painted moon-dial in the arch, a chime/silent lever and the usual seconds pointer and a date-ring at the base of the dial centre. Winding of the going-train

A,B,C Lantern clock weights of lead, of various shapes.
D Pear-shaped lead weight from a lantern clock alarm train.
E Lead weight used on early types of long-case clock.
F Brass-cased weight of the type used on early clocks of high-quality, particularly London-made ones.
G,H Two iron weights generally associated with white-dial clocks.
I Cast-iron weight showing the weight cast into its upper surface. This would be intended for a 30-hour clock.
J Cast-iron weight, one of a pair intended for eight-day clock use. Its weight, 12 lbs, is cast into the bottom surface.

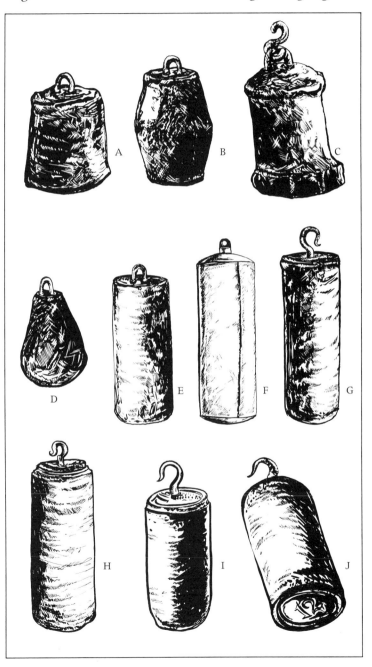

is done through the centre of the calendar-hand, whose mounting-pipe, or cannon, had been made especially large to allow this facility on a crowded dial.

One of the most neglected areas in writing of old clocks is that of the weights, whose constant and unaltered pull help to give the long-case clock its reputation as a timekeeper. We have dealt with the expected weight on clocks going for various durations except to say that 7 lb is the normal weight for a going and striking 30-hour clock. The very first weights used on domestic clocks were made of lead. Like most things of this period, individual shapes are met with and weights were often round chubby lumps of lead, or they could be eight-sided or sometimes pear-shaped. The very first long-case clocks were equipped with cylindrically-shaped lead weights, and the higher quality clocks, which meant many of them towards the end of the 17th century, were encased in brass. These were carefully made with domed tops incorporating a cross-drilled boss at the top of fixing the suspension hook. Generally these tops are screwed on to an iron centre-rod in the weight by a female thread in the previously mentioned boss. Lantern clocks and 30-hour clocks almost always retained the basic lead weight. Provincial clocks are rarely seen with brass-encased weights as an original feature. The high-quality, eight-day and longer duration clocks usually have rather long cylindrical weights. With the increased production of clocks, and the manufacture of parts in factories, the clock weight received its share of attention. We therefore expect a white-dial clock to be driven by cast-iron weights, though I have no doubt that some did begin life with lead weights and some late brass-dialled clocks with iron weights. Large flat hooks were generally cast into the iron variety whereas lead weights often had an unbroken iron staple cast into their tops for suspension by a wire hook attached to the weight-pulley. Some iron weights are seen with their weight cast into the surface. This is found on the top rim or sometimes on the bottom, where it is more likely to be large and in the centre, protruding rather than in inverted form. On an eight-day clock, where a pair of weights were involved, one is often seen to be larger than the other although matching in other details. The larger weight goes to the strike train. Many clocks are over-weighted and a well-adjusted eight-day clock in good order may be found to run perfectly well on a 4 lb weight. The 12 lbs to 16 lbs which is normally found, will keep the clock running long after it should have stopped for attention. This is one of the reasons why so many clocks that have been used regularly are considerably worn.

Chapter 7

Bracket clocks

Portability was one of the most attractive features of the bracket clock. It could be carried from room to room and used on a side-table or stood on the mantle-piece, as its less commonly used alternative name of mantle-clock implies. In many examples the bracket clock was more of a jewel than the long-case clock. This was not just because of its size but its decoration was frequently more elaborate and the extra work involved in the making of reliable springs to drive it was extremely costly. It was partly these two factors of expense and the very considerable difficulty in drawing out reliable steel springs which made the bracket clock a rarity in provincial centres at an early date. The spring would not give an even pull to the clock. It was particularly strong when newly-wound but not so vigorous when running down. As a result a special feature was developed to overcome this problem of unevenness in the spring-action. This device is known as the fusée, found in all good English spring-driven clock and watch work. The principle involved in this mechanism is one of ratios, as in a variable gearbox; but the spring barrel and the fusée are not directly linked except by the line which is wound from the spring barrel to the fusée in winding and in the opposite direction as the clock runs. The spring inside the barrel is arranged to remain partially wound even when all the line is back onto the barrel and the clock is wound down. This is necessary to keep the line in tension or it will fall off the barrel and onto the arbor, causing great problems at each winding time. In 19th-century bracket-clock work a finely pitched roller-chain or a twisted wire line replaces the more traditional gut-line used in the 17th and 18th century work. Even with this sophisticated device, rates of timekeeping never equalled those obtained with the constant weights and the long pendulum of the long-case clock.

It was for portability and reliability that the bracket clock retained its use of the verge escapement long after it became obsolete for good timekeeping. The reasons are similar to those given in the chapter on lantern alarm clocks: a clock which

might be stood on a rickety tripod table or an uneven mantle-shelf needs to be fairly insensitive to levels. Clocks were made by sophisticated London makers and others with the verge escapement and bob-pendulum as late as 1780. The short bob-pendulum directly linked to the pallet-arbor did not have to be used with the verge escapement. Early high-quality examples are found with provision on the dial for making the clock go slower or faster. This is done by turning a hand which is set in a sub-dial. The pendulum could be raised or lowered from its point of suspension by leverage controlled by this adjustable hand. The pendulum therefore had to be suspended from this lever by a flat spring, and control the escapement via a crutch, just as the long pendulum does in long-case work. An elaborate and heavy clock, perhaps situated permanently on the mantle-piece, could therefore have its pendulum adjusted for time-keeping from the front. Otherwise there would be the incon-venience of lifting the clock down to open the back door. From about 1690 until approximately 1740 the mock pendulum was used as a decorative feature on the dial's centre. This showed

91 *Left:* An ebony chiming bracket clock by Tompion and Banger, London, clock no 92. The dial plate is an upright oblong shape, to accommodate the two sub-dials at the top; circa 1710.

92 *Right:* Movement of a bracket clock by Henry Jones, circa 1680. The verge escapement and bob pendulum, as well as the pull-repeat mechanism can clearly be seen.

through a lunette-shaped slot of about $2\frac{1}{2}''$ cut in the dial-plate, immediately beneath the figure twelve. This small disc, often engraved with a sunburst design, was directly connected to the pallet-arbor by a wire and monitored the action of the pendulum. It is sometimes stated that this device allowed one to see at a glance if the clock was going. This is hardly necessary, for its characteristic noisy click is unmistakeable.

As in other types, the earliest striking bracket clocks used the method of count-wheel strike. Mounted externally on the backplate these count-wheels tended to be rather small and placed high, to the right of the plate. Many bracket clocks did not have a strike-train but were made with a pull repeating facility for bedroom use. Others had both an hour-strike and the repeat-work, which was usually the type known as quarter-repeat, making use of two bells. The deeper-pitched bell struck the hours and on the higher, one blow indicated each quarter passed. The principal of a snail and a gathered rack was first used in bracket clocks to facilitate this pull quarter-repeat and later it was used for the conventional hour-strike-train as well. When used in pull-repeat work the rack was made without a tail. An extension on the end of the toothed rack butted against the snail and was gathered up not by a single-toothed pallet but by a pinion with six or more leaves. The action of pulling the repeat-cord both wound the spring which gave the power and forced the rack-extension against the edge of the snail. When the cord was released the rack was wound back by the pinion to strike the appropriate hour and quarter. Since the amount of the rack's movement towards the snail depended upon the hour, it can be seen that the cord could not be pulled quite so far at one o'clock as it could at twelve o'clock. In later bracket clocks, using the conventional rack-and-snail method of strike, the snail was mounted independently of the hour-wheel and changed by a star-wheel in one positive action just before the warning for the next hour. This provided accuracy when using the strike rack to repeat the previous hours. The example shown in Plate 94 works as an hour-repeater in this way. This example on a long-case clock dated about 1740 is extremely unusual for the feature is rarely found outside bracket-clock work.

The repeat facility does not seem to have been used quite so much during the last quarter of the 18th century, when the anchor escapement became a regular feature in bracket clock movements. The elaborate repeat and strike work which was found early in the century was abandoned. Most bracket clocks were now made with a simple hour-strike.

Musical-trains were found in bracket clocks more regularly than in long-case work and also had their more popular period earlier. Most were made in the second quarter of the 18th century. These worked in just the same way as described in the chapter on long-case clocks but were driven by a strong spring and not a weight. Occasionally musical-trains also operated automated figures in the dial-arch. These were frequently musicians or dancers for the tunes played were often marches, jigs or minuets.

Since it was an achievement to operate the clock at all with the springs available, bracket clocks which go for longer than eight days are extremely rare. One magnificent year clock was made by Thomas Tompion for William III. This clock struck the hours and also incorporated a repeating facility. The spring barrels and fusées needed to run the clock are so large that they took up three-quarters of the total space of the movement, and the wheels and pinions of the rest of the trains are extremely delicately constructed.

The fully-blown bracket clock was a showpiece of superb craftsmanship, and above all it provided a focus for the engraver's skills. Backplates came to be highly decorated in

93 *Left:* Another view of the movement by Henry Jones (Plate 92), showing the rack-and-snail arrangement, used as a pull quarter-repeater.

94 *Right:* Long-case clock movement (eight-day) by James Woolley of Codnor. The strike snail is mounted on a twelve-toothed star-wheel. This is advanced by a pin (hidden) in twelve distinct movements, to give increased accuracy in striking of the last hour in repeat work. This feature is unusual in a long-case clock, but was frequently used in bracket clocks.

126

95 Anonymous bracket clock backplate, with fine rococo engraving. The bob-pendulum is seen hooked to one side for carrying.

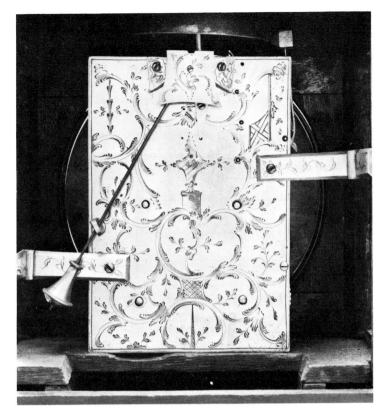

this way. At first, in the late 1660s and 1670s, the engraving was restricted to the count-wheel whose centre was usually engraved with a Tudor Rose. On some fine examples each hour was numerically engraved beneath the appropriate slot. The backplate was decorated only with the maker's name. By the 1680s floral and foliate engraving spread over the backplate and was enclosed by an engraved line close to the plate's edge. The maker's name continued to appear in an engraved cartouche in the lower central area and, on some clocks, not on the dial at all. The overall decoration continued on most examples and styles developed with the taste in vogue. Examples with foliage arabesques from 1700 will often be found enclosed by a wheat ear or herringbone border while in Rococo examples in the mid-18th century, the shapes are free and unbounded except by the limits of the plate. Highly decorated and exaggeratedly shaped back-cock covers were fitted in clocks between 1680 and 1700. The practical purpose of these was to hold the rear of the pallet-arbor into its V-slot, but they were developed into intricately engraved and pierced decoration. An example of work of this period is shown by Plate 92 on a clock by Henry Jones. Circular clock plates are

127

96 *Left*: Circular bracket clock plates engraved in the neo-classical taste, from the clock by Stewart of Glasgow, circa 1795, shown in Plate 98. This clock is controlled by an anchor escapement. Temple Newsam House, Leeds.

97 *Opposite*: Bracket clock by John Cloues of London with an extremely fine basket top.

98 *Page 130*: Satinwood bracket clock, by James Stewart, Glasgow, circa 1795. The case is inlaid with tulip wood and holly. Temple Newsam House, Leeds.

99 *Page 131*: English cartel wall-clock in carved and gilded wooden case. Movement by James Gibbs, London, around 1760. Lady Lever Art Gallery, Port Sunlight.

highly unusual on English clocks, but are clearly an obvious choice when the movement is fitted into the upper part of a narrow-waisted, balloon-shaped clock such as the one shown from Gillows' estimate books (Plate 65) and the example shown here by Stewart of Glasgow (Plate 98). This clock dates from about 1795 and has an anchor-escapement and hour-strike of the rack variety. While the layout is conventional enough, the design and finish is superb, a great deal of thought having been given to the engraved backplate and positioning of the bell, even though the back door is not glazed. The engraving is seen to be in the neo-classical taste which was popular with decorators at this time.

The movement and case of these clocks can be seen to have very little contact when viewed from the back and sides, though firm fixing is essential if the clock is to be reliable. The clock by Henry Jones shows how the oblong movement-plates sit on strips of oak in the case bottom. Two square-headed screws pass upwards from underneath the case and into threaded holes cross-drilled into the bottom two movement

130

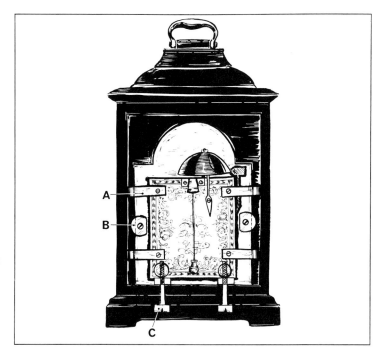

Right: Methods of fixing a bracket clock into its case:
A Right-angled metal straps screwed to backplate and case sides.
B Circular discs with one flat side. These are fixed to the back of the dial and are shown in the locked position with the round edge turned into a slot in the case. To remove, the flat side is turned toward these slots thus releasing the dial from the case. These are principally used on early clocks, in association with C.
C Large screws which come from beneath the case and fix into threaded holes in the bottom two movement pillars.

100 *Opposite above:* 18th-century wheel-cutting engine by Thomas Green of Liverpool. The concentric rings of holes for dividing the teeth and the peg used to measure out the number of teeth required on the wheel, are clearly shown. Craven Museum, Skipton, on loan from the Rector and Church Wardens of Carlton Parish Church.

101 *Opposite:* A modern method of wheel cutting using a small lathe fitted with a dividing attachment (left); fly cutter on the vertical slide (right).

pillars. This fixing is very firm but occasionally augmented by a rotary latch at each side of the back of the dial-plate. This is an ingenious little device which will be better understood by means of the drawing above. Slightly later and possibly introduced initially for heavier and more complicated movements was the right-angled or elbowed bracket; this was screwed to the backplate and also the inside of the case. The screws passed from the outside of the case to a threaded hole in the elbowed bracket. At first these were used in conjunction with pillar-screws through the base. On later clocks these were used as the sole means of fixing the movement to the case, and were engraved to match the backplate.

In order to stabilise the bob-pendulum while carrying the clock, a hooked device was normally fitted to the backplate of the movement. Since the wire pendulum rod is usually somewhat flexible, the pendulum could be sprung into this hook, where it would safely stay. Later clocks with pendulums hung from a suspension spring needed an even more rigid fastening and this was achieved by fixing a block to the backplate which was slotted to the width of the pendulum rod. A broad-headed screw could be screwed into the block next to the pendulum rod which trapped the rod firmly while travelling. When the clock was in action, the screw could be placed safely out of the way by screwing it into a specially provided hole in one of the movement fixing brackets.

Chapter 8

Wall clocks

This chapter deals with clocks made to hang on the wall. It was never really a very popular area once the lantern-clock period had passed. Possibly this was something to do with the difficulty of suspending heavy movements and weights when a long-case clock could be had that would easily stand on the floor and take up very little extra room. Early examples were weight-driven and from the mid-18th century clocks driven by springs were introduced.

Mention has already been made in the chapter on lantern clocks of the hooded wall clocks made at the end of the 17th century. Constructed like a long-case clock in most respects but with no trunk, these cases were mainly in walnut, with or without marquetry inlay. A decorative carved under-structure on the bracket supported what was virtually a smaller version of the long-case clock hood. The weights – one or two depending on whether it was an eight-day or 30-hour clock – were always on view, generally cased in brass to enhance their appearance. These clocks may have had one or two hands, or be of plate or posted construction, and long-pendulum or verge-pendulum control. Few were made in comparison to other types and they are now so rare that today's collector may almost disregard them.

During the early years of the 18th century a large wall-hung, weight-driven clock was developed for use in public buildings. This is known as an Act of Parliament clock, after an Act of 1797 which imposed a stiff tax on ownership of clocks and watches. Clocks were charged with an annual tax of five shillings. This tax, similar to the one imposed on house windows, was soon seen to be unwise and was repealed after only nine months. During its period of enforcement however, people were said to have hidden, or in some way disposed of, their clocks and pocket watches, relying on the large Act of Parliament clocks provided in inns. We know that clocks of this type had been made for at least 80 years before the Act and so, although providing a horological reminiscence of an unpopular parliamentary decision, the name is not very accurate.

102 Tavern clock by William Scafe, London, circa 1760. This is a large clock and should have a sweeping centre seconds hand, which has been temporarily removed. The principal hands are not original; the movement is shown in Plate 105. Temple Newsam House, Leeds.

These clocks were used in a variety of public places. They are recorded in churches, chapels and in the corridors and kitchens of country houses, but their main use seems to have been as tavern clocks and I think we should favour this name for historical accuracy.

Some coaching inns did have lofty rooms even at the end of the 17th century and tavern clocks would have been hung high up in a prominent place. The earliest known clock of this type has a japanned case and eight-sided dial surround, with inscribed on a curious carved medallion below the clock: 'The Gift of Sir Frances Forbes 1714'. Unfortunately it is not known for what purpose the clock was made.

The predominant feature of the tavern clock is its large dial compared to its short case body, which is just long enough to accommodate a seconds pendulum. Since visibility was the important factor this is to be expected. Dials were as large as 30″ in diameter and were virtually made as part of the case. To start with they were made of wood. Oak was frequently used for the dials, which were constructed of two or three pieces or planks placed vertically side-by-side and butt-jointed and reinforced with cross-members at the back. Case bodies and decorative features were usually made in pine. The finish of the majority of the clocks up to about 1780 was black japan work. The lettering and dial work were in gold on the black ground, and decorative detail frequently was inspired by the oriental, although always japanned in this country. The door of the trunk was usually treated pictorially and these pictures often give a clue to the original use of the clock. The clock by William Scafe illustrated in Plate 102 shows three men in European dress, seated at a table drinking. Above this scene and providing a japanned border to the arched door are bunches of grapes. Carved ornaments at top and bottom of this case also have the grape as their subject, indicating that this clock was made for a tavern. A late tavern clock by Moore of Ipswich makes use of a montage of figures made up of coloured engravings on its door. Paper prints were cut out and stuck on to make a picture depicting an English tavern scene. That this is original work seems to be in no doubt since it is bordered by gold lines and varnished in, taking on the same patination and age as the rest of the case.

Most of us can recognise tavern clocks from their large dials and small bodies but their silhouettes can vary radically. The first examples had octagonal edges to their dial frames but had round painted rings, indicating the minute and other markings. A half-round wooden bead formed decoration along this octagonal edge. This shape of dial proved a favourite and

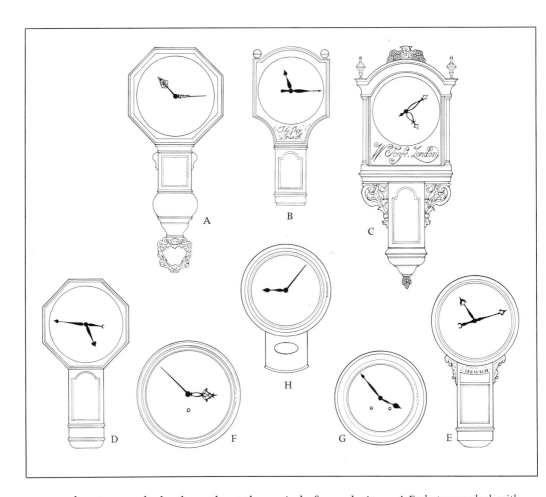

A Early tavern clock with octagonal dial, circa 1714.
B Straight-sided dial with arched top, circa 1755.
C Elaborate case with carved decoration and brackets under the lower squared edge of the dial, circa 1760.
D A simple octagonal-dial tavern clock, circa 1770.
E Round-dialled tavern clock with decorative brackets, circa 1770-80.
F Early English dial with well-proportioned case. Late 18th early 19th century.
G Later English dial with less pleasing lines. Mid-late 19th century.
H English drop dial. Late 19th century.

occurred on tavern clocks throughout the period of popularity (drawing A). Another early style was a straight-sided dial with an arched top, with the bottom corners of the dial area cut away to provide a smooth flow between the line of the dial and the case (as in B). Some kept the base of their dials square and had fretted ear-pieces or brackets to provide the same visual flow into the line of the trunk (drawing C). A re-occurrence of the octagonal dial is shown in D, this time with a plain parallel trunk to the case and the whole of the case front taken up by the arch-topped door. The style using a round dial and parallel case trunk shown in drawing E dates from about 1770-80 and was of the later type. Occasionally, these were made in pine and veneered in mahogany.

In many ways the dials of tavern clocks are reminiscent of the dials of church-tower clocks, with their plank construction and gold-leaf number work. Also the way in which the dial is presented, with its surface unprotected by glass or a cover of any sort. As a result the clock needed to be hung high out of

103 Unusual anonymous tavern clock dated 1776. This clock has a single counterbalanced hand. The case has been altered, and made longer in order to increase the duration between windings. The clock was designed as a pull-wind 30-hour clock.

reach of interferring hands. Early dials were usually written in gold on a black ground and after about 1770 a white ground was used for the dial, lettered in black. This, however, is not a firm rule, for on the previously-mentioned clock inscribed 'the gift of Sir Francis Forbes' the lettering was written in black on white, and it has more finely detailed brass hands than later clocks do. Polished brass hands were used throughout and these were fairly simple and frequently matching in the same way as on a long-case clock, the minute-hand being an elongated form of the hour-hand. A favourite device for terminating the counter-balanced end of the minute-hand was a crescent moon.

The clockmaker's name or signature was a prominent feature of the tavern clock's design and was written in large flowing gilt script, sometimes as much as 4″ high. On the earlier and middle period clocks this is usually to be found in the area of the dial, underneath the 30-minute marker. Usually the name of the town was written in the same flowing script. Later tavern clocks are generally found to have the signature painted on the trunk, just below the rim of the dial. When this is the case the trunk door top is convex, to afford the space and the letters are similarly placed to echo this convex arrangement. The maker's name continues to be written in script but the town is often found in capital letters of a less flowing type. To call these timekeepers clocks is not strictly accurate as they were invariably without a striking-train. The reason for this is not hard to find. We have already mentioned the difficulty of fixing a heavy clock and large lead weights to the wall. The weight needed to drive these clocks for eight days (the normal duration) was heavier than that in a long-case clock because the cases only allow the weight a very short fall. To compensate for this, an extra wheel was needed, making five in the train; and this required additional weight to drive it. The hands too were larger than usual. So large, in fact, that a counter-balanced design of minute-hand was always used, to reduce the drag imposed on the movement in lifting the hands. Sometimes the hour-hand was decoratively counterbalanced too and very occasionally one also sees a centre seconds hand. The high-quality movement shown in Plate 105 is from the tavern clock by Wm. Scafe, London, in about 1760 and shows that it has its escape-wheel placed in line with the hand pipes, with the escape arbor extended through the centre of these to provide a drive for centre seconds work. The minute work is geared from the second wheel of the unusual hour-wheel train, between the plates, while the hour pipe is driven from the same arbor but

via a gear squared on to it, outside the main plates. The movement is fixed to the back of the dial by four wooden screws from the brass fixing plate attached to the front of the movement. While this fixing plate is laid in a horizontal plane to the vertical arrangement of the movement plates, its front surface is partially scribed and laid out with the same unusual wheel arrangement as the clock. This was obviously intended as the front plate, before being discarded, turned on its side and then used as an earlier form of the later iron false plate used to connect some white dials to their movements. The wheel work and design for the pillars is London work of high quality. The weight needed to drive this sturdy train is 18 lbs. Because of this centre seconds feature and the larger number of teeth in the wheels, the movement of this clock is unusually large, having plates measuring $6\frac{1}{2}'' \times 4\frac{3}{4}''$, more like the plates found on an eight-day striking clock. The single train of a tavern clock could easily be incorporated in plates much smaller than this and usually were. A reduction was made in their width, leaving the plates parallel, though long and thin in proportion.

The usual way of mounting a movement in these cases was to sit it on a wooden seatboard built at a suitable height inside the case. The dial, which was detachable, was not directly connected to the movement but to the sides of the case trunk. Holes for the hand pipes and winding arbor were made to coincide.

104 English dial with single train, shown from behind with the case backbox removed.

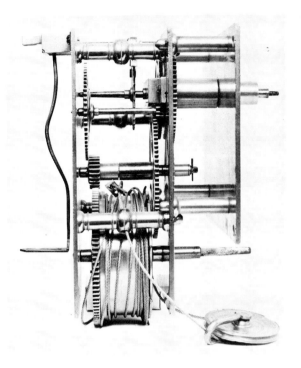

105 *Left:* The movement from the tavern clock by William Scafe shown by Plate 102. The escape-wheel arbor extends through the hour and minute pipes to provide an attachment for the centre seconds hand. Temple Newsam House, Leeds.

106 *Right:* Fine-quality English striking movement from a drop dial clock. The matching hands and false plate for dial fixing are clearly visible.

The clocks are generally deep enough back to front to accommodate cylindrical weights, but even so the weight would have to be quite long to achieve the correct weight. This was not desirable in a short case and a wide, oval weight was used. These weights were usually brass-cased, although lead ones are also seen.

The tavern clock was regional in its manufacture and was much more common in London, the Home Counties and East Anglia than anywhere else. It was, indeed, a clock of the south of England; I know of no such clock made in the north and cannot recall seeing one made in the west country though I do not doubt that some may exist.

Clues to the next development in wall clocks can be seen in drawing E on page 136. Small versions of these clocks were made at the end of the 18th century. They have mahogany cases and metal dials with a glass cover edged by a brass bezel. Weight-driven movements were not so convenient as the now improved spring-driven variety and spring-driven movements were used in increasing numbers. In early clocks which used a verge escapement and a bob-pendulum, the trunk of the case was often dispensed with, giving the simple circular silhouette of the English dial clock. In examples using the anchor-escapement and a slightly longer pendulum, the trunk was retained in shortened form. This style of clock is known as a drop dial. The two case styles persisted throughout the 19th century into the early years of the 20th century. Few early verge escapement examples were made, and are rarely seen today except in specialist dealers' shops where they fetch a high price. Delicate wooden rims, usually in mahogany, denote earlier examples, as do refined and gracefully written dials. Some clocks of quality had engraved and silvered dials just like their larger counterparts, the long-case clock. Hands were well-made and frequently of the matching variety, cut in steel and given a blued finish. Early painted examples had a gentle convex curve to their iron dial-plate and its covering glass. Movements were fixed to the back of the dials by false plates and could be lifted clear of the box at the back. This enclosed the movement and kept it free of dust. The box was quickly refixed by four wooden pegs which were pushed through bearers at the back of the dial-frame and into the sides of the box. A door at the bottom of the box, and often one at each side, was provided for lifting in the pendulum and fixing it in position. With the weight problem no longer a consideration, some of these spring-driven clocks included an hour striking-train, which, like most English clocks, struck the hours only on a bell. Perhaps three-quarters of those made did not strike.

Gradually there was the inevitable coarsening of the product. The style was found to be convenient for offices, public buildings and eventually schools, railway waiting rooms, Post Offices and so on. Many thousands were produced and mass-production meant a lowering of aesthetic standards. Cases now were often made in oak, broader in the rim and no so attractively finished as the early mahogany examples. Flat dials were painted with graceless numbers and given solid, stumpy hands. The strong, craftsman-made English fusée movements continued to be made throughout most of the 19th century, however, and to a high standard; a lot of them can be found today in first-rate condition. A clock of the late type which feels light when lifted should be examined carefully as many later English dials enclose a German mass-produced movement of considerably inferior quality.

Cartel clocks must be dealt with separately for although they were made concurrently with the tavern clock from about 1740 they were not made in great numbers in this country. They were a product for the luxury end of the market and probably made as a result of the inspiration of decorators rather than the clockmaker. The cases of English-made examples were usually carved in wood; pine was the first choice for carving, although limewood or other suitable soft woods may have been used.

107 Opposite: Black Forest novelty clock, surmounted by a carved and painted wooden figure which eats plums. P. Dickinson of Preston would be merely the retailer. Late 19th century or possible even 20th century.

140

141

108 *Opposite:* Musical organ clock by George Pyke, London, circa 1765. This clock is also shown in Plates 47 and 123. Temple Newsam House, Leeds.

109 *Right:* A view of the clockmaker's shop in Abbey House Museum, Kirkstall, Leeds. Hanging on the wall (top left) can be seen two English dial clocks. The large bracket clock in the foreground is a late 19th century chiming clock loosely based on an 18th century style. In the background is a mahogany North Country long-case clock, circa 1840.

These were then coated with gesso and gilded. Most of those which survive are enriched with carved designs in the rococo taste. The designs closely resemble those incorporated in frames of looking-glasses and on candle-sconces. Frequently these designs contain oriental details and are often surmounted by a bird with outstretched wings resembling the Chinese 'ho-ho' bird. Chippendale's ideas were successfully uses as a basis for some of these fantastic cases.

There is nothing unusual about the spring-driven English movements used in cartel clocks, which were of the verge pendulum variety with a short bob pendulum. This type of movement fitted more easily into the small area available at the back of the case, and was easy to set up since it was the least sensitive to level placing. Dials were always of the single-piece brass-sheet type, circular and delicately engraved with nothing more than the necessary chapters, minute markings and the maker's name and town of origin. Few are known that were not made in London. Striking trains, calendars, and so on are absent, though the concaved false-pendulum lunette is a common feature and is situated, as in all verge clocks incorporing this feature, between the dial centre and the Roman twelve which marks the hour. Hands made of steel conform to bracket-clock types of the period 1760-70, during which these clocks were most popular. They have a minute pointer and a cross-over loop pattern of hour hands. Winding was naturally done from the front and if the clock had been allowed to stop, the pendulum could be set in motion by pushing the false pendulum. The dial was covered by a glass and the customary hinged brass bezel.

Chapter 9

Mass-produced and novelty clocks

In this chapter I shall attempt to cover some of the many types of old, though not necessarily antique, clocks which might be found by the second-hand and antique-shop browser today. Not all are English clocks, but they all have played a part in the story of English clockmaking, are still with us in this country and are part of the cheaper range of the clock-collecting scene.

Towards the middle of the 19th century the growing demand for house clocks was answered in part by the cheaply-imported American clocks known as shelf-clocks. They were imported in vast numbers and were successful not only for their cheap price but also because the basically hand-crafted English product could not be produced in sufficient numbers to satisfy demand. American manufacturers such as Eli Terry and Chauncey Jerome had made a study of factory methods of inexpensively producing clocks in the early 19th century and were able to flood the English market with these at a cost so low that many people thought they had been purposely under-valued to corner the market. Many are seen today and will be recognised to be of two main types. The smaller has a steeply pointed top which was known as the Gothic case. This was made in pine and veneered in rich red mahogany. The glass door takes up most of the frontage and is usually divided half-way by a glazing bar, again mahogany veneered. Dials, made of thin sheet zinc, were fragile and thinly painted. Their shape either echoed the shape of the Gothic top or was circular. A painted area in the manner of the glass gilder's art almost always decorated the lower glass door panel, and inside the case a large label was pasted to the backboard proclaiming the maker's name, the nature of the product, and sometimes included a small drawing of the clock factory. The label was laid out in grand style in the manner of a 19th-century playbill. The Gothic-topped clock was usually under 18″ high. The larger version of shelf-clock was often square-topped, with the entire case front bordered by a wide, shallow concaved moulding giving the appearance of a Victorian photograph frame. The same glass door, dial and label were typical, though a square

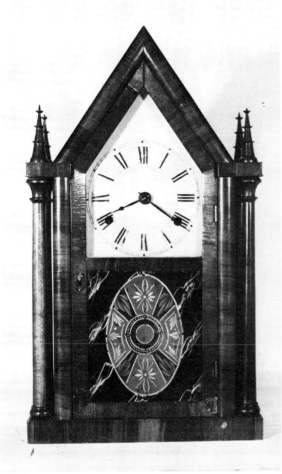

110 *Left:* American shelf clock with Gothic case. American Clock and Watch Museum, Bristol, Connecticut.

111 *Right:* A Black Forest clock of the 'postman's alarm' style which was extremely popular in Britain in the 19th century.

dial was always used in these cases. At first movements were weight-driven and to make the most of the shallow drop available the lines were taken upwards and looped over pulleys in the 'roof' of the case before turning downward to weights which were directly hung and fell either side of the movement. Later clocks are almost all spring-driven and of the 30-hour variety. The movements appear light and spidery with skeleton plates and thin gauge wheels. A form of count-wheel striking may operate on a bell or gong screwed into the back of the case. These clocks may have been masterpieces of early mass-production – and are recognised for that – but they are little regarded today for any other reason.

German clocks, made cheaply in the Black Forest region, joined the American shelf clocks in flooding the English market. Together they aided the demise of the English handcraft trade, which was never again to enjoy the eminence it had at the end of the 18th century, when thousands of clocks were made to traditional high standards. The Black Forest clocks came in many types, most of which are seen quite regularly today. These vary from large cuckoo-clocks to the round dialled postman's alarm with its white or mauve enamelled dial. The cuckoo-clocks are traditionally in wooden chalet cases decorated with carved birds and branches. These can be very attractive but if the cuckoo, leather bellows, or any of the lantern pinions are damaged, they can be very time-consuming and frustrating to repair. Other German clocks include a wall clock without a case but with an arched wooden dial, shaped almost like that on an English long-case clock. The dials are made of softwood, and quite thick, about $\frac{5}{8}''$ being the usual thickness. Heavily filled on the front and brightly painted with flowers and leaves in a primitive manner, they are reminiscent of the gypsy art of waggon or canal longboat painting. Bright colours were used and the brushwork was direct and unsophisticated. Both these wall clocks and the postman's alarm type, made especially for the English trade, bore the same type of heavy cast brass hands of a matching pattern incorporating a diamond-shaped area near the tip. This is pierced with a circular hole. Weight-driven movement frames were principally of wood, and on very early cuckoo clocks the wheels may have been too. Some Black Forest shelf clocks were made by factory methods and had brass spring driven movements so that at first sight they greatly resemble the American shelf clock of the same period. This may have been a deliberate ploy to capture a share of the Americans' trade which was undercutting German trade and helping to destroy the English industry. Thick, stubby wooden arbors typified much of the Black Forest output when wheels were cut from brass and pinions of the lantern type were made from iron wire. Frame cross pieces and so on were made from wood and only pivots and bushes were made in iron and brass. The wooden frames were so bulkily made that little in the way of doors was needed to make the movement dust tight. It is on these clocks that we first see iron weights cast in the shape of fir cones. These weights and the carved cuckoo-clocks are not to be confused with the later products, much smaller and of diminished quality, which still form a mainstay of the German tourist souvenir trade.

One of the most sought-after clocks is the type known generally as a Vienna or Vienna regulator. This is a general and broad term of reference, for the original Vienna regulators were made from the early 19th century, and many examples are late and cheaper German and occasionally American copies. These

112 German-type, Vienna regulator with the strike train by Gustav Becker; late 19th century.

are wall clocks about 3′ 6″ long; the cases have glass side panels and a full-length glass door. The early regulator was restrained in its design and had a going train only; it was made by hand as a precise timekeeper in the finest possible way. In their execution and delicate construction these Austrian movements were nearest in quality to the French clock movements of about the same time. Many later Vienna types had an additional train which struck the hours and a single blow at the half hour, on a curled gong-type spring fastened into the back of the case. The movements were secured by sliding them into a cast brass bracket fastened to the backboard of the case, to which was also hung the suspension for the pendulum. This was made from a flat length of painted soft wood, reinforced by brass, in the slot provided for engagement with the pin of the pendulum crutch. A large spun brass bob, usually backed with zinc, and a rating nut completed the arrangement. Fine gut lines supported the delicate brass-cased weights of about $4\frac{1}{2}$ lbs which are a distinct feature of the style.

Cases were at first simple but beautifully made. Constructed in stained beech and softwood, the backboard and details were usually veneered in walnut although the finer early type of case was sometimes blackened in imitation of ebony. Art Nouveau sometimes influenced case design, with a wavy silhouette. These also are generally of the true regulator type with going train only. Ultimately the product was cheapened, and over-elaborate German copies with highly decorated cases were produced in great numbers. Decoration was in the form of applied split turnings and carved cresting, terminating top and bottom in turned wooden finials or a German eagle. Enamelled dials which had previously been of a single piece were often now made in two pieces and held together by a thin pressed brass central rim; half-hour decorations were sometimes seen in red. The main chapters retained their black colouring but increased in size and became less refined. Later still the case was shortened and debased in line even further. The weight-driven movement gave way to a spring-driven version and the Americans also began to produce the style. One of the clues to immediate recognition of a late Vienna regulator is the pendulum. Smaller than before, it was made to look like a compensated grid-iron pendulum. The bob with an enamel centre often carries the letters A and R, indicating the direction in which the rating nut would need to be turned in advancing or retarding the timekeeping of the clock. The Gustav Becker factory was a leading maker of German Vienna-type weight- and spring-driven clocks. Their products are frequently found and

147

the movement can be recognised by the stamped mark G.B. and the design of an anchor in a medallion on the backplates of the movement.

Not all the clocks mentioned in this chapter were cheaply made. We have already mentioned the Austrian Vienna regulator which was certainly a high-quality product, and some English makers continued to produce bracket clocks and smaller mantle clocks as a cross between the bracket clock and a French carriage clock to cater for the better end of the market. One style of English clock which became quite popular towards the third quarter of the 19th century and which was usually extremely well made was the skeleton clock. These were spring-driven table clocks whose plates were cut away in loops and scrolls so that a full view of the wheels in the train and the workings of the escapement could be clearly seen. In order to protect the movement from dust they were always covered with an oval glass dome. Most skeleton clocks were unsigned but the expert can recognise many of their makers by the style and shape of the plates. The skeleton clock was originally a French idea and it was developed there almost a hundred years before the type was made in England. English clocks are in-

113 *Left*: English skeleton clock in the Gothic style, with the glass dome removed; circa 1860.

114 *Right*: French mysterieuse clock with gilt bronze figure holding the pendulum; circa 1875. Victoria and Albert Museum, London.

clined to be more decorative than the French examples, which were often on elegant neoclassical lines. Perhaps the fact that English skeleton clocks, like many other pieces of furniture and furnishing from the Victorian period, became so fussy has limited their appeal to many clock collectors. The inventiveness of the clockmaker is evident in many examples, though, more in the decoration than in the timekeeping features. In rare examples unusual escapements are seen and occasionally a striking train is included, although most popular skeleton clocks were made with one train only, using the English style of spring barrel with a fusée, a four-wheel train, and a recoil anchor escapement. A single blow at the hour was usually struck by a halberd-shaped hammer on the bell situated at the apex of the frame. This was done by the passing strike method, whereby the hammer tail is picked up and dropped on the hour by a single pin placed on the reverse minute wheel.

By far the most interesting feature of skeleton clocks is the variety of plate shapes that are seen. The type just described often makes use of a simple scroll design. The scrolls may simply terminate in turned-under enlargements through which the plate pillars are usually screwed or they may be cut to resemble leaves or even shaped in a Chinese style to resemble a pagoda. The shape of a lyre is used as a basis for some clock plate forms. Cathedral styles were copied for some clocks and in these examples a strike train and sometimes a chiming train is usually found since the architectural style provided scope for a wider frame. York Minster is recognisable as a basis of some clock plate designs, as is Lichfield Cathedral with its characteristic three spires. The Scott Memorial in Edinburgh featured as an inspiration for the plates of a skeleton clock designed and made by the W. F. Evans factory in Birmingham for the Great Exhibition in 1851.

Dials used on these clocks were of two main types. The earlier type was a simple enamelled ring in the French style. Used with plain hands often of a Breuget pattern with ring decoration near the tip or a simple spade design. In my view this was the best method, providing a simple contrast to the scrolled plates and giving a clear indication of the position of the hands. Better-quality clocks too used a simple ring of brass, engraved and silvered with a similar visual effect to the French enamelled style. Rare signed skeleton clocks often have this type of dial. Later on dials too were fully skeletonised to the extent of having only a series of twelve shields held together with ribbons of brass. Produced in the same way as the plates, these were cast and hand finished before being engraved. Frequently their

Blake**b**orough,

WATCH AND CLOCK MAKER,

Jeweller, Silversmith, and Ironmonger,

Grateful for the liberal Support which he has experienced for many Years, begs Leave to inform the Inhabitants of Otley and its Environs, that he

CONTINUES TO SELL THE FOLLOWING ARTICLES,

At Reduced Prices:

Watches, Plain and Patent, Horizontal, &c. Clocks of all descriptions.
Gold Watch Chains, Seals, and Keys.
Gold Broaches, Ear Rings, and Hoops.
Necklaces and Wedding Rings of Standard Gold.
Gold, Gilt, and Silver Snaps.
Gilt and Jet Necklaces.
Black Ear Rings, Broaches, and coloured Beads of all Kinds.
Silver, Gilt, Steel, and Bead Purses.
Gilt Watch Chains, Seals, and Keys.
Gold, Gilt, and Silver Clasps and Buckles.
Silver, Tortoise-shell, Gilt, Plain, Japanned, and Tinned Snuff Boxes.
Patent Thimbles, Gold and Tortoise-shell.
Silver Pints, Gills, and Cream Jugs.
Table and Tea Spoons, Sugar Tongs, Caddy Spoons, Thimbles, Pencil Cases, and Punch Ladles.
Plated Tankards, Pints, Cups, Table and Tea Spoons.
Candlesticks do. with Silver Mountings.
Castors in Sets, Spurs and Toast Racks.
Spectacles, Silver, Tortoise-shell, and Steel Frames.
Combs, Tortoise-shell and Steel, of all Sizes.
Toilet Combs, Ivory, Small Tooth, do. and Pocket Combs, with proper Handles.
Leather Pocket Books, Thread Cases, Purses, Work Boxes, &c.
Fifes, Flutes, Violin Strings, Walking Sticks and Canes.
Mahogany Swing Looking Glasses.
Do. Hanging do.
Pier Glasses, in Gilt Frames.
Sykes' Patent Powder Flasks, Shot Belts.
Guns, double and single Barrel.
Pistols do. do. and Flint.
Ladies' Pelisse Clasps, do. Gilt, or Steel. Do. Shoe Clasps.

Spring Roasting Jacks, Brass and Japanned Cases. Cranes.
Copper Scales and Beams. Beams of all Sizes.
Weights. Butchers' Troues.
Tea Trays, Paper and Japanned.
Metal Tea Pots, Table and Tea Spoons.
Tea Caddies and Tea Chests.
Japanned Bread Baskets, Waiters, and Chamber Candlesticks.
Brass and Iron Candlesticks.
Knives, with Ivory Handles, and Carvers to match.
Dessert do. do.
Knives, with Stag and Pressed Handles.
Pocket and Penknives. Razors.
Scissors of all Kinds.
Wool Shears. Patent do.
Patent and Common Cork Screws.
Sugar Nippers.
Snuffers and Snuffer Trays.
Black Lead Pencils.
Copper and Iron Coal Boxes.
Copper Tea Kettles, Sauce Pans, Warming Pans, &c.
Patent and Common Umbrellas.
Parasols. Fishing Tackle. Best Glue.
Ladies' Fancy Ridicules.
Marble and Spar Ornaments.
Weather Glasses. Prospect Glasses.
Patent Balances, for weighing Sovereigns and Half Sovereigns.
Lamp Black, Emery, Crocus, Pumice Stone, &c.
Brass Cocks and Air Vents for Barrels.
Rat and Mouse Traps, Wire, Toys.
Warren's Real Japan Blacking.
Brass Pans, of all Sizes.
Knockers for Doors.
Rasps and Files of various Kinds.
Locks and Hinges of all Kinds.
Stringing and Shells, for enlaying.
Brass and Polished Steel Fenders.
Green Fenders, with Brass Tops & Balls.

Kitchen do.
Polished and Common Fire Irons.
Box and Solid Irons.
Bellows.
Brushes, Broom Heads, and Chamber Brushes.
Carpet, Bannister, and Hearth Brushes.
Flat and Round Whiteners.
Best Painters.
Stove and Shoe Brushes.
Bottle Brushes.
Hair and Tooth do. &c. &c.
Black and Bright Augurs, Gimblets.
Do. and do. Hammers.
Masons' Trowels.
Smoothing Planes, Jack Planes.
Short Trying do. Long Trying do.
Bead do.
Nails of all Sorts.
Hand, Pannel, and Ripping Saws.
Dovetail and Tenor do.
Butcher's do.
Cast Steel Patent Scythes and Sickles.
Cast Steel Chisels and Gouges.
Do. Garden and Turnip Hoes.
Cast Steel Plane Irons.
All Kinds of Tires for Carpenters, Joiners, &c.
Commodes, Knobs, Escutcheons, Locks, and Keys.
Hinges and Screws, Bells, Curtain Pins, Rings, Brass Nails, &c.

Castings.

Ranges, Stoves, Ovens, and Boilers.
Hearth Grates, Pots, and, Pans.
Baking Plates, Frying Pans, &c. &c.

In addition to the above List, R. B. has very recently received a fresh Supply of Hardware, Jewellery, Silver, and Plated Goods, too numerous for insertion.

R. B. cleans and carefully repairs Clocks and Watches of every description; also Weather Glasses, Bottle Jacks, Silver Plate, &c.

THE BEST PRICES GIVEN FOR OLD GOLD AND SILVER.

EDWARD BAINES, PRINTER, LEEDS.

150

115 Label from the case of a clock by Richard Blakeborough of Otley, circa 1830. A telling document for the English clock industry.

style was so florid that it produced a confusion with the plates and wheels and made it difficult to see the time shown by the hands. Skeleton clocks were screwed to their base by bolts extending downwards from the feet. The bases were most usually wood, but marble was sometimes used. The edges of the base were usually grooved to accommodate the large glass dome.

French clocks with their characteristic round movements and dials are also seen in quite large numbers. A characteristic of the clock is usually its decorative gilt metal case. Earlier and good-quality French clocks to be found have cases of bronze or gilding metal but many of the poorer mass-produced clocks made throughout the late 19th century and even the early 20th century were of a brittle grey metal alloy known as spelter. The light weight of such a clock and the poor aesthetic quality of the sculptured figures will usually give a good guide in identifying the type – though it should be said that almost all French movements are of lovely quality even at this period.

Mysterieuse clocks involving a sculptured female figure standing on a rock base above the movement and dial of the clock, and holding the pendulum in her outstretched arm, are a feature of late French work. So also are marble-cased clocks, whose pendulum action takes the form of a child seated on a rocking swing. In the latter case the pendulum action is normally arranged to have backwards and forwards motion instead of side-to-side swing, and in the former the pendulum is kept moving by a tiny oscillation of the figure, it is impossible to see until pointed out. This style was copied by the Americans, although the quality of such pieces is usually inferior.

Novelty clocks were made by most nationalities and in many case materials, though animated figures in carved wood are often found to be of German origin. The 19th-century plum-eater timepiece pictured in Plate 107 is of Black Forest origin and is thought to have been used as an advertising feature for a restaurant. The winding arbors extend both backwards and forwards so that winding may also take place from the back.

From the early 19th century an international variety of inexpensive clocks was available in England and little call was made upon the average English provincial clockmaker to actually make a clock from raw materials. Much of his day would be taken up with repairs and the selling of imported clocks, leaving time to become a stockist of a host of other artefacts loosely connected with the trade. A long-case clock by R. Blakeborough of Otley numbered 2343, and dated about 1830, has pasted inside the trunk door a large label measuring 11″ by $8\frac{1}{2}$″ and giving us an excellent picture of the period (opposite).

Chapter 10

Some notable clockmakers

In writing on makers of repute I have not concentrated on the most famous, listing only the names of London makers of the decades either side of 1700, as some works do. Instead I have written about a number of men whose work was original, spirited and typical of the time in which they were active. All made a contribution to the English horological tradition, with fine clocks of various types. It is only possible to write with conviction about the things which one experiences and this has influenced my choice of makers here. I have been lucky enough to work on the clocks of some of them myself. Others, clearly could not be left out, because of their eminence in the field. In the space available, there must be a limit to the makers mentioned, and I therefore have restricted myself to the very personal choice below.

Ahasuerus Fromanteel (1607-93) is perhaps a suitable man with whom to begin since his claim to have made the first pendulum clocks in this country has not been refuted. The extract from his advertisement proclaiming this fact has been quoted on page 93; it suggests that he had probably also made the first clocks which went for one year at a single winding. His work was of the finest quality and he was a pioneer, making many of the very first bob-pendulum long-case clocks. Few examples by any other makers survive. It is clear from reading about the man that he preferred his work as a clockmaker and the environs of his workshop to honours and office in the Clockmakers' Company. He did not restrict his inventive powers only to clocks. In addition to the pendulum referred to in the advertisement on 28th October 1658 in the *Mercurius Politicus*, he goes on:
'There is also by the same Ahasuerus Fromanteel, Engins made in a new way of his own invention for quenching of fire, which have been thoroughly proved, and found to be effective, whereby those that use them are not deceived in their expectation; for that they are not subject to choak with Mire, and when they are clogged with Dirt, may be

thoroughly cleansed without charge, in half a quarter of an hours time, and fit to work again. Neither are they without extreme violence broken and by reason of their smalness, may be wraught where there is but little room; and some be so small, that they may be carried up an ordinary stairs in a house, and there used; And are very serviceable for washing Vermin off the Trees, and Hops, and for the watering of Gardens, and Cloths, and the like.'

The industrious nature of the man and the advanced ideas of his workshop made him the focus of a group of makers at this time, some of whom were related to him. Lantern clocks survive by one Andrew Prime, a London clockmaker who was married to Fromanteel's sister Elizabeth. Thomas Loomes, another early maker of lantern clocks, married Fromanteel's daughter Mary in 1654. His sons, John, born in 1638 who went to Holland and worked in Salomon Coster's workshop, Ahasuerus II, born in 1640, and Abraham, born in about 1646, were all clockmakers and so too was his stepson Joshua Winnock. It is hardly surprising that of the few surviving early lantern clocks many are by members of this family or their associates, for they were probably the largest group and certainly the earliest working in London on domestic clocks. The Fromanteel workshop was in Mosses Alley, Southwark, and later at the Sign of the Mermaid in Lothbury, which was the home of Thomas Loomes. The Mermaid had formerly been the home of John and William Selwood. A lantern clock by William Selwood is shown in Plate 23. Thomas Loomes was a Selwood apprentice and when the two died, John in 1651 and William in 1653, Thomas Loomes took over as master of the workshop. Close family and craft ties meant that Fromanteel did some of his work there and it is certainly likely that Thomas Loomes worked on many pieces bearing the more famous Fromanteel name. Ahaseurus I, lived to a good age, dying aged 86 years in 1693. As he aged, it seems likely that his sons played an increasing part in the family business. Abraham spent a good deal of his working life in Newcastle-upon-Tyne and died there in 1730, the last surviving member of the direct line.

Thomas Tompion (1639-1713) is often proclaimed as the father of English clockmaking. His skill as an innovator and as a manufacturer of clocks is perhaps second to none, exceptingperhaps Ahasuerus Fromanteel who by his work laid the foundations of the craft in England and provided the basic ideas which Tompion's inventive genius and incredible craft skill were able to develop. Tompion was famous for the range of these skills: he carried out experimental work on escapements, made observatory clocks, exquisitely tasteful and well-proportioned house clocks, and complicated bracket clocks with repeat work and quarter-chiming. Some of these were so small and detailed that they defy description. Watches too received his attention and his speciality was in making watches with a repeating facility. In all Tompion made about 6,000 watches and about 550 clocks. He was among the first to adopt division of labour in his workshop, using up-to-date machines such as the wheel cutting engine to speed production. A number of workman apprentices and servants lived at the Dial and Three Crowns off Fleet Street which was Tompion's house and workship combined. It is thought that he was the busiest craftsman of his time, and a clock or watch by him was then and certainly is now, a most treasured possession. As you would expect in such an organised and methodical man, his products were carefully numbered. From this numbering system we are able to tell a great deal, and date the bulk of his surviving output fairly accurately. He died in 1713 and is buried in Westminister Abbey.

John Harrison (1693-1776). You will probably never see a domestic clock by John Harrison for very few examples exist. He was an unconventional figure of the horological scene, giving up most of his working life to the development of the marine chronometer. He was born in 1693 near Nostell Priory in Yorkshire, where his father worked on the estate as a carpenter and by 1700 the family had moved to Barrow in Lincolnshire. He became fascinated by clockwork and made examples in wood, which was the material he obviously knew best, using oak, lignum vitae and box for his frames, wheels and pinions. Some metal was used for pinions and pivots, but surprisingly little. Lignum vitae is a hardwood and lasts well when used as a revolving surface. At this time repairing clocks was probably John Harrison's main work and would probably have remained so had he not heard of the government's offer of a prize for a maritime timekeeper in about 1726. Precise navigation was essential to a maritime nation and it required an accurate timekeeper. The problems were enormous, for a conventional pendulum could not be used at sea, and in vessels sailing long distances, varying temperatures and atmospheres would also create errors unless these could be compensated for. In 1714, believing the sea clock almost impossible to make, the government set up the Longitude Board and announced a prize of £10,000 to anyone who could make a clock accurate enough to within one degree on a voyage from England to the West Indies and back, £15,000 to within two-thirds of a degree and £20,000

116 *Right:* Miniature bracket clock by Thomas Tompion. Timepiece only with a 4½″ square dial and pull-repeat on two bells; circa 1695. Fitzwilliam Museum, Cambridge.

117 *Far right:* John Harrison's marine chronometer 'H4'. National Maritime Museum, London, on loan from the Ministry of Defence (Navy).

to within half a degree. In 1728 Harrison visited London and it is thought that he discussed the idea of making a sea clock with George Graham, who encouraged him to do so. By this time he had already invented the gridiron pendulum and also the complicated but accurate escapement with pivoted pallet arms known as the 'grasshopper' escapement because of the sudden jumping action of its arms.

Back in Barrow, Harrison set to work on the longitude problem and eventually produced a sea clock with a grasshopper escapement, a pair of linked balances, and other revolutionary ideas which would allow the clock to keep going in spite of the movement of the sea. Bringing the marine timekeeper, or chronometer as it came to be called, with him John Harrison moved to London in 1735. A sea test was arranged by the Board on a voyage to Lisbon, with Halley the Astronomer Royal and George Graham the clockmaker aboard to observe. The clock did so well that at the end of the voyage the Board granted Harrison an advance of £500 to assist with the development of the work. A second clock was ready by 1739. Like the first one, this too was a heavy machine using balances terminating in heavy brass balls to counteract the movement of the ship. A grasshopper escapement and a spring connected by a fusée to the wheel train was used. Since England was at war with Spain sea trials were not possible as it was unthinkable that such a valuable instrument should fall into the hands of the enemy. The Board allowed Harrison a further small advance and he continued his work, making a third machine. In 1757 he considered the third large clock ready for a sea trial, but asked the Board to wait until he had completed a watch with which he could make a cross-check on the performance of the clock. The watch, which was virtually a large and very refined verge watch with a compensated bi-metal balance, exceeded his expectations as a timekeeper and it was decided that the watch itself should be tested in place of the third sea-clock. Eventually in 1761 William Harrison, the son, set sail on H.M.S. Deptford with the watch to Jamaica. John Harrison, who by now was an old man, stayed at home. The return trip was an outstanding success. During the five months away, the watch lost only one minute and 53 seconds, equivalent to less than half a degree longitude. Harrison had after almost 40 years of work fulfilled the conditions needed to win the Longitudes Board's prize of £20,000. However, the Board decided that his impressive performance was perhaps a fluke and they would like another trial. Further delays followed and the second sea trial took place in 1764, when the watch was taken to Barbados and back. The results confirmed the excellence of the watch and they were even more impressive on this occasion. In five months the corrected error was in order of 54 seconds, well within the conditions of the Board's specifications. There were still more delays in paying out the prize and the Board decided that this would not be done until Harrison had described and drawn the watch and demonstrated its ideas to a panel of six members of the Board, and Nevil Maskelyne the Astronomer Royal. One member of this panel was the London watchmaker Larcum Kendall. Eventually it was decided that a copy of Harrison's watch should be made, but by now Harrison was becoming embittered. Not only had he not been given the prize money which he so rightly deserved but he had to give up his watch in order for it to be copied by Kendall, and Kendall was paid £450 in advance to do the work. The watch K1 was a splendid piece of work and even William Harrison said that in terms of workmanship and finish it was a better product than the original. K1 was completed in 1769 and delivered to the board in 1770. Its first big test came shortly afterwards when it accompanied Captain Cook to the South Seas. After much wrangling and disgraceful behaviour by the Board of Longitude, an appeal was made to the King to get Harrison the remainder of his prize. This was finally paid over in 1773; just in time, for Harrison, whose sight was already failing, died in 1776.

John Williamson (d. 1748) and **William Tipling** (d. 1712), makers at Leeds. In writing on these two makers together I am hoping to throw light on a link between them, which, although undocumented, is suggested by the similarity in their work. Their's was typical high-quality work carried out in a provincial centre (Leeds) at the end of the 17th century and the beginning of the 18th century, and bears all the hallmarks of an original and highly skilled workshop. Williamson's name occurs on a year clock, two-month clocks and two eight-day clocks, all of which are known to me. He was not a run-of-the-mill maker of provincial 30-hour clocks. All those mentioned are cased in walnut, parquetry, and marquetry cases. All their known clocks are long-case clocks, although other types may remain undiscovered. Both men signed their dials similarly at the base of the dial plate and used the forms 'John Williamson at Leeds Fecit' and 'William Tipling in Leeds Fecit' or very similar variations. The engraving on each dial appears to be by the same hand. Certainly their dials were inspired by the same man and were almost certainly from the same workshop.

The layout of the movements too appear to derive from the same workshop design book. Dates available suggest that Tipling, the younger man, may have been apprenticed to John Williamson, although I have no proof of this. In 1682 a John Williamson was recorded as being a member of the London Clockmakers' Company, which would account for the quality of his training. A man of this name is recorded as marrying Rebecca Whalley in Leeds, on 5th December 1683, and it seems probable that this is the clockmaker for the Leeds clocks by John Williamson date from about this time. A young man, newly married and setting up business as a clockmaker in a northern city would require an apprentice. William Tipling married Ruth Norton at St John's Chapel on 10th April 1692; in 1683 he could have been a boy of the right age to be apprenticed to Williamson. From 1692 onwards it seems likely that Tipling set up his own business, continuing to make quality clocks in the manner of his training. At this period Tipling lived at Bridgegate (Briggate) and Williamson lived at Hillhouse Bank. Williamson lived a long and productive life, having made some superb clocks; he also married three times and had fourteen children. Pre-deceased by his third wife, he died in the work-house in 1748 a very old man. Tipling on the other hand died young. He seems to have had a maintenance contract for the clock and bells at St. John's Church in Leeds, where he worked from 1694. In 1701 he received a payment of 10 shillings as his annual salary, and he died in 1712.

Henry Hindley of York (1701-71) was a clockmaker whose contribution to horology and engineering has recently been re-evaluated. After recognition in his lifetime, and shortly afterwards, his importance seems to have gone unnoticed until fairly recently. Though Henry Hindley's name is associated with

118 The signature of Henry Hindley while at Wigan.

119 *Opposite left:* Marquetry-cased eight-day clock by John Williamson of Leeds, circa 1695.

120 *Opposite right:* Superb ball-moon long-case clock by Thomas Ogden of Halifax, circa 1760.

York where he spent most of his working life, his birth and apprenticeship were in Lancashire, possibly Manchester. Little, however, is known about this period of his life, but at least one clock signed Hindley de Wigan and made during the period 1725-30 is known. This clock bears many of the features associated with his style, along with bolt-and-shutter maintaining power and a $1\frac{1}{4}$-seconds pendulum. He moved to York as a fully trained young man in 1730 or 1731 where he set up in business as a clockmaker. As well as possessing horological skills, he was a clever engineer making many of his own tools, engines and scientific instruments for others. His renowned wheel-cutting engine made before 1741 was considered to be the best ever made and appears to have been an instrument of precision and refinement involving some very fine gear-cutting. He also developed a device for accurate cutting of fusées, used in spring-driven clockwork. He made a large tower clock for York Minster in 1750 at a cost of £300. Bracket clocks of a unique type and involving many advance features were also made. The making of bracket clocks in itself was fairly unusual, for they are extremely rare from Yorkshire makers in the 18th century. Hindley thought out every part of his work for himself and there is not doubt that he was a brilliant and inventive man. Recognisable Hindley features in a clock movement include fine gear-cutting and high numbering of his wheels and pinions, crossed-out ends to the weight clock winding barrels and knee or L-shaped blade springs to the hammers. He developed an early type of dead-beat escapement and made year-going and revolving ball moon clocks.

George Pyke (apprenticed 1739). The inspiration for including this note on George Pyke, who was active in London during the mid-18th century, is his imposing pedestal organ clock at Temple Newsam House, Yorkshire, illustrated by Plate 108.

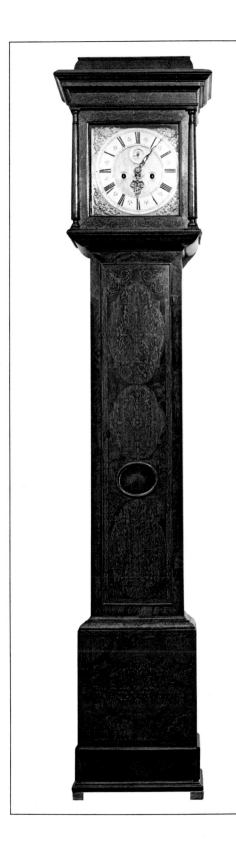

121 *Opposite:* Hooded wall-clock of about 1680, with an eight-day striking movement. British Museum, London.

John Pyke, his father, was a clockmaker of some eminence, but George was perhaps less so and is now remembered particularly for his automated organ clocks, a number of which survive. Both father and son were interested in making clocks with automated features and musical work, and it is thought that this interest stems from work that the elder Pyke did to complete a musical pedestal clock after the death of Charles Clay in 1740. Clay had made a number of similar clocks throughout his career and can be said to be the originator of the style, although it seems that most of Clay's musical clocks played on bells. One made in 1736, exhibited before the Queen and ultimately sold by a raffle, incorporated bells which were played by a weight-driven mechanism. The George Pyke organ clock and others known can be said to represent the mature culmination of the same style. It is detailed both in its outward appearance and the complication of its working parts. The peninsular cornered base, veneered in ebony, is hollow and gives space for the descent of the massive weight, needed to drive the organ pin-barrel and provide wind for its pipes. Plate 47 shows the dial proper and the large dial plate which is in various phases to allow for the animated figures articulated by complicated motion work via a gear-drive from the organ mechanism. These are activated three-hourly when the organ plays.

The clock mechanism is a conventional English bracket fusée movement with anchor escapement and hour striking independent of the organ. The organ consists of three registers, two of pine and one of tin, each of twenty pipes tuned at 8, 4 and 2 ft pitch governed by three manual stops (flute, principal and piccolo). There are eight tunes, selected on a numbered dial at the side. There is also an 'off/play' pointer. Two sheepskin leather bellows are pumped by a connecting rod attached to an extended 8" flywheel, the whole being driven by a massive lead weight descending into the pedestal. The music is discharged every three hours:

Pretty Polly Hopkins
Drops of Brandy
Unidentified
Life Let us Cherish
Mrs. Whitmore
Why ever don't you come
Bergere Legere (Manimet)
Sicilian Mariner's Hymn

The tune selection dial is engraved by the maker George Pyke, Bedford Row, London, and the sound board is inscribed March 1765.

James Woolley, Codnor, Derbyshire (c. 1700-86). That James Woolley made superb high-quality long-case clocks there is no doubt. Most of the stories of him, however, refer to his miserly attitude and to his eccentric behaviour. It is said that he was caught poaching on a nearby estate when quite young and having paid the penalty vowed to work non-stop until he had acquired his own estate on which to shoot 'without dreading the frowns of his haughty neighbours'. By work and thrift he seems to have achieved this and more and when he died in 1786 he had amassed a considerable fortune.

James Woolley is thought to have been apprenticed to the Nottingham clockmaker John Wild. A clause in Woolley's will substantiates this idea to some degree for he left to 'the two children of John Wyld Watchmaker, Deceased and grandchildren of the late John Wyld clockmaker of Nottingham the sum of five pounds each'. Baillie's *Watch and Clockmakers of the World* lists John Wild of Nottingham as about 1780 but by this time he must have been long dead.

The first mention of a clock by James Woolley is from the diary of a Lincolnshire farmer giving the date 1724 and recording the purchase of a square, oak clock from Woolley of Codnor at Derby Market for £4.10s.0d. although Woolley had asked £5 for it. Shortly afterwards Woolley gave a clock for use in the New Exchange Hall at Nottingham. This hall was almost built in 1724 and from all accounts the clock appears to have been a turret clock with a dial on the front of the building. The account from *Hanes Every Day Book*, Vol. II, of 1827 reads as follows: 'Once in his life Woolley was convicted of liberality. He had at great labour and expense of time made what he considered, a clock of considerable value, and as it was probably too large for common purposes, he presented it to the Corporation of Nottingham, for the Exchange. In return he was made a freeman of the town 1728. They could not have con-

122 Dial from a long-case clock by James Woolley of Codnor, Derbyshire, circa 1740. It has especially fine hands and an unusual calendar. Its movement is shown in Plate 94.

123 *Left:* Musical organ clock by George Pyke with hood removed. The clock movement cannot be seen, but wheels which activate figures on the dial are visible on the left. The large toothed wheel behind the tune-selector disc is fixed on the end of the pin barrel; the fly wheel and linkage to the bellows are in front and beneath this. Organ pipes are ranged at the back of the clock to the right. Temple Newsam House, Leeds.

124 *Right:* Thirty-hour movement of Will Snow's 473. The hammer tail and the pins which lift it can be clearly seen bottom right.

ferred on him a greater favour; the honour mattered not – but election dinners were things which powerfully appealed through his stomach to his heart. The first he attended was productive of a ludicrous incident. His shabby and vagrant appearance nearly excluded him from the scene of good eating, and even when the burgesses sat down to table, no-one seemed disposed to accommodate the miserly old gentlemen with a seat. The chairs were quickly filled; having no time to lose, he crept under the table and thrusting up his head forced himself violently into one, but not before he had received some heavy blows on the skull.' The clock was in regular use until 1881.

At first it may be difficult identifying authorship of a clock by James Woolley for he frequently signed his dials 'Wolley Codnor', giving the impression that this was a complete name. No explanation is offered for this oddity in dropping one of the Os from his surname; Codnor is the name of the village where he lived. Some of his clocks were occasionally signed James Wolley of Codnor Fecit. It seems he was something of a specialist in repeating strike work, for of the three clocks by him that I noted, all have pull-repeat work and two have a precise quarter-repeating facility on two bells. In each case the gearing of the strike-train has been given extra duration to account for this. The clock illustrated in

Plate 94 is an hour-repeater only but uses a star-wheel method of advancing the rack, for greater accuracy and a more precise change. The steel work is well detailed in all his movements and the terminals of various features are filed and carved in the manner of a gunsmith. He is also known to have used as a decorative feature a rocking dove, with olive branch, before an engraved ark, in the arch of a long-case clock. It is not known who made his clock cases but a firm quality and a sophisticated line is evident in their construction. An early 10″ square-dialled long-case clock is recorded in an ebonised case. The one illustrated in Plate 94 is in a heavy solid oak case and another is recorded in oak with walnut crossbanding. The dial shown in Plate 122 can be dated about 1740 and is of good classic line though unusual in one or two respects. The use of a hand and an engraved applied ring for calendar work is early; generally this feature is found on white-dial clocks of the late-18th century. The curious cast satyr head decorations at either side of the seconds dial are unusual but pleasing. I have seen them on clocks by other makers but only rarely. The hands, in common with all other steel work, are of the finest quality.

125 Thirty-hour clock by Thomas Ogden, circa 1750, with a Halifax moon. The hour hand is not original.

James Woolley died, a very old man, in November 1786, and in his will left a considerable portion of his large estate including farms and houses to John Woolley his nephew. John Woolley was also a clockmaker but perhaps due to his inherited wealth and consequent lack of drive did not make as many or as good-quality clocks as his uncle had done. His works are signed, variously Jno Wooley Codnor, John Wooley Codnor, or Woolley Codnor, and they are often clearly from a later period than James Woolley's clocks. John Woolley died in March 1795 aged 57 years.

Thomas Ogden of Halifax (1693-1769) was a second-generation clockmaker of an ardently Quaker family. Branches of this family spread north and made clocks in Alnwick and Newcastle, but Thomas Ogden stayed in Halifax and became its finest clockmaker. His speciality was in moon-dial clocks and he was a successful exponent of the revolving-ball moon dial type of work, making many fine examples. This uncommon feature is often mistakenly called a Halifax moon. The true Halifax moon which is illustrated by Plate 125 was often used by the town's many clockmakers in the 18th century, but was in fact originated much earlier and was seen on some of the work of the Fromanteel family at the end of the 17th century. From contemporary writings, Thomas Ogden comes down to us as a rather straight and somewhat patriarchal Old Testament character. His obituary notice in the Leeds Mercury 1769 confirms

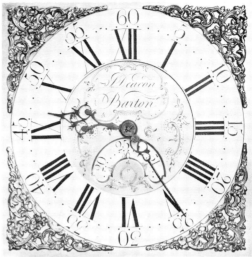

126 *Left:* Octagonal dial of an extremely fine eight-day clock by Thomas Ogden of Halifax, circa 1750.

127 *Right:* Thirty-hour long-case clock dial, Sam Deacon's No 44.

this estimate of his character. 'On Thursday last October 3rd died in his 77 year of his age, Mr. Thomas Ogden of Halifax, clock and watchmaker. His superior abilities in his profession are sufficiently well known in this and some neighbouring counties. A great many gentleman's houses being furnished with the productions of his labours. He was one of the people called Quakers. His moderation and charity to all other religious sects was truely exemplary. His peculiar diction in the Epistolatory Style made his correspondence greatly desirable by everyone who had any connection with, many of his epistles, being preserved on the closets of the learned and curious. He was a steady friend and a facetious companion compassionate and indulgent, a great promoter of industrious merit, but a severe scourge to the slothful and indolent. He died without issue, and he left his fortune to a numerous train of relations.'

A man with firm views, he was fond of legends about the passage of time and Man's mortality. The following are typical of those found engraved on his dials. *Tempus edox rerum* (Time devourer of all things) and *Memor brevis esto aevi* (Be mindful of thy short life).

On a long-case timepiece made early in his career for the Northgate End Unitarian Chapel, Halifax, he used the following Latin phrase to decorate the four spandrel corners instead of cast decorations. *Fugit hora ora labora* (The hour flies pray labour). A fine eight-day long-case clock with an arched dial recently seen, surprised me by having no moon work. Engraved on a tablet in the dial arch was the instruction 'Wind me on Monday'. Thomas Ogden was also a maker of watches;

but these are rarely come across these days. It seems unlikely that he made many. The frontispiece illustrates what must be his finest ball-moon clock known to exist. It is signed 'Thos Ogden de Halifax'. I have seen three others but the movements, though on the same lines, are not so fine. Plate 120 shows a perfect specimen of his work in its original mahogany case which has Lancashire and possible Gillows characteristics.

Samuel Deacon of Barton in the Beans, Leicestershire (1746-1816). Sam Deacon, clockmaker of Barton, has come to prominence recently not for his outstanding skills (and he was a capable and comprehensive maker of clocks and watches) but for the discovery in 1951 of his virtually intact workshop by John Daniells of the Leicestershire Museum. Samuel's son John Deacon was also a clockmaker and, when his father died, carried on working in the family workshop though he concentrated on making up movements for Birmingham dials and later using both dials and movements, bought in from Birmingham factors. John's son, also Samuel, succeeded his father but was principally engaged in repairing and not making clocks. It is thought that the workshop was idle from the mid-19th century but the property and adjoining house were retained by members of the Deacon family until 1951. When the family moved away, Mr Daniells was allowed to look round the outbuildings and found the amazingly complete 18th-century workshop as set up by Sam Deacon in 1771. The tools and equipment gave an insight into the scope of Samuel's work and the working life of a country clockmaker at this time. On the ground floor was the forge complete with large bellows, and upstairs in the workshop proper were found the old wooden benches, vices, a lathe and a wheel-cutting engine. There was also a testing frame of wood on which the movements were tried out before fitting to their long cases. A separate area was partitioned off for making watches and barometers. The most important find, however, was the account books and workshop records, which begin in 1771 and end long after Samuel's death in 1860. The books tell us much about the work, the costs and the selling price of the clocks as well as domestic accounts and information relating to Deacon's interest in the Baptist Church of which he was a deacon and an active local preacher.

Deacon's 30-hour clocks appear to have been cheaply made, with small movement plates and plain parallel turned pillars. They frequently incorporate a curious form of internal countwheel, pinned instead of slotted for its division. Plate 127 shows a clock of this type, No. 44, dated 1773. Some of his eight-day clocks, however, including No. 338 of 1789, have much fine

128 Front plate showing the marking out of the trains. Sam Deacon's No 44, made in December 1773. It can be seen from this plate that the escape-wheel pivot hole is worn oval and is badly in need of bushing.

decorative work including eccentric baluster-turned pillars and a steel rack-hook, shaped and engraved to look like a bird. It seems that Samuel Deacon's work could vary to suit the requirements of his market and could do work as good as most.

William Snow of Padside, near Pateley Bridge, Yorks (1736-95). Clocks by William Snow will not be known nationwide, but a few will almost certainly have removed to other parts of the country with their owners. As far as is known Will Snow was a first-generation clockmaker and no information exists about his training, although he was followed in the clockmaking trade by three sons, William, Richard and Thomas. Will Snow was probably foremost a hill farmer and used clockmaking to occupy the winter months and supplement his income. Generally clocks by him are of the 30-hour country variety and I have never heard of an eight-day clock or any other type. The movements of these clocks are very unusual because of their simplicity. Plates are cut away in rectangular skeleton form in order to save material. Pillars are normally a piece of parallel round steel bar with no decorative turning. The normal bridge or back cock to retain the escapement arbor is dispensed with, the arbor being assembled in with the plates. The cock for suspending the pendulum is simply a length of steel rod riveted into the backplate. Both one and two hands were used and following the normal pattern the single-hand variety tend to be earliest. Dials of 11″ square vary little, but are tastefully laid out and nicely engraved, the centre with lunette calendar and scrolling leaf engraving. This area was usually silvered along with the chapter-ring. Hands were nicely made and conform to the style of the period. In fact all the visible and dial parts of his clocks suggest a delicacy not expected from a country maker working in relative isolation. A pleasing touch occurs in the signature, as a result of Will Snow's fortunate habit of numbering his work. Engraved on to the chapter ring, the number usually follows the name and often leads to him including an 'S' after Snow. Thus we see Will Snow's 660. I like to think that the possessive S is a proud touch, and indeed the man had much to be proud of for if his numbering system is accurate he produced up to 900 clocks in a busy life. From the clocks that are dated, and the general distribution of the numbers seen and recorded, we are able to assume that Will Snow aided by his family made an average of 25 clocks a year. After Will's death his three sons continued making clocks separately in nearby market towns. These are of the white-dial variety. The last son died towards the middle of the 19th century.

Chapter 11

Buying and restoring clocks

The Clock may be sett up by any carefull Carpenter if he attends to the following directions: having taken off the lid of the packing case, let him then take out the weights, ball and keys which are in the corners at the Case Head, also take out the bars of wood which go across the Clock Case and which are fastened by screws on the outside of the packing Case: he will then take out the Clock Case, and set it carefully in the place it is to stand in: this being done, he may open the Clock Case door, and set the body of the Clock case as perpendicular as he can, by a plumb line both in front and at the side (in this part of the business he should be very attentive, as the well going of the Clock depends upon it) he should then fix the case by screwing it fast with two screws screwed thro' the back as high as he can get them for the door, as also two below, as low as he can get for the door also: perhaps it may so turn out that he cannot find a place in the wall to hold the screws mentioned if so should prepare two pieces of wood and fix them to the Wall and then screw the case to them. All this done he will find a piece of wood unscrewed . . . pendulum ball with two screws this he must take off by unscrewing . . . he will then find a piece of wood screwed behind the pendulum ball, these screws he will also take out, and by drawing the pendulum ball gently and carefully forward, he may take the piece of wood from behind it: he may then hang on the weights and set the clock a going. The smaller weight hangs under three o'clock and the larger under nine o'clock.

The Clock is at present very near time, but perhaps some little derangement may take place by the Carriage and if it should be found to go too fast or too slow it may be brought to time by screwing up the small ball of the pendulum which is below the large ball to make it go faster, or down to make it go slower and one turn will alter the rate of the clock one second per day—below the regulating ball is a small nut which should always be kept close to the ball to keep it in its situation.

Left: Notes for setting up the long-case clock by John Holmes, bought by Godfrey Wentworth of Woolley Hall, Wakefield in 1794.

If you have bought a clock or have spent any time looking round antique shops checking on the prices and condition of those offered for sale you will already have formed some opinions and maybe gained a little knowledge. Not all will be about clocks. Very few dealers have a thorough knowledge of clocks and many of them make no secret of the fact, simply offering the clock for sale at a fair profit and in much the same condition that they bought it in. Others, sadly, will spin you a yarn about its pedigree, its restoration and often accompany these half-truths with a story or two. In either case you will need to have the knowledge yourself or be able to take someone along who really does understand old clocks. An illustration of this latter breed of dealer is shown by my experiences some years ago when a friend approached me to look at a small pretty mahogany long-case clock that he wished to buy. The price was fairly high, but the clock certainly looked attractive in its well-polished case, standing beneath a spotlight in the shop window. I removed the hood and looked at the clock thoroughly, taking in features such as a hardboard surround to the dial and nuts and bolts soldered to the dial to hold it to the movement. What we were looking at was a clock made from various pieces, all of about the same age but put together unskilfully, exposing the deceit. Its condition suggested that this clock had recently been 'got up' for sale. Wishing to advise my friend of this fact and not wanting to cause offence to the attentive and pushing salesman, I awaited an opportunity that never came. Instead I was trapped in conversation and was forced to either go along with his inaccurate appraisal of the clock or call his bluff. I tried to do this politely and suggested that hardboard was not a natural material for the 18th century cabinet-maker, nor were dials normally held on with nuts and bolts. The conversation became more and more heated, and when he realised the sale was no longer possible, the salesman informed me in no uncertain manner that I was no longer welcome and that he did not care for people who knew everything, showing us both the door as he did so. Salerooms can also be a problem area for people with little knowledge. It is not easy to be sure about a clock on a crowded view day and the clock need not even be a good one to make it attractive to people who are prepared to pay a high price. The atmosphere of the sale will possibly be infectious, causing the unwary to go too far and pay a ridiculous price.

The best way to acquire an old clock is to inherit it, for at least one does not feel cheated if it turns out to be not quite right and sentiment can often make up for any deficiency in its

originality or condition. Unfortunately this method of acqui-
sition can be ordered by few of us; undoubtedly the next best
method is to visit a specialist dealer. Anyone who specialises in
clocks has usually a good selection on display in restored and
working condition, and is likely to know something about
what he sells and be prepared to back his descriptions, as well
as the clock's condition with a guarantee. Talk to the dealer, tell
him what you are looking for and get him to show one or two
examples of his stock and tell you about their age, the maker
and even the restoration that has been necessary to present the
clock in good condition. A dealer who is truly interested in his
stock and know about it will be pleased to do these things,
providing he recognises that you are not wasting his time. In
buying a clock from such a man there will be no bargains, but at
least you will know that you have got what you have paid for.
The dealer's profit will usually take account of the amount the
clock's value will probably rise in about twelve months, but
after this period the clock should be worth more than you paid
for it. A further safeguard, in addition to dealing with a reputable and experienced man, would be to have a second opinion;
so if you can, take along with you a restorer or person with a
good knowledge of the subject. Book knowledge can also be
gained, for there are many excellent books on the market today. This does, however, need to be supplemented by actually
seeing clocks for there are certain areas which are not always
clear to those with knowledge, and even experts disagree.

The word 'fake' is one not commonly associated with clocks.
At least it is not a word that I have heard used recently. The
tone of intentional deceit conjured up by this word does not
often apply to the clock market today. Few if any clocks are
made from the outset to imitate a valuable old clock in the hope
of gaining a massive sale-room price. It would in most cases cost
as much to do this as the genuine clock would be worth. In the
past, names were altered on chapter-rings and dials but it was
often done unskilfully and in a way which fools no-one with a
reasonable knowledge. Faking of this sort went on when less
well-known makers had the names of the famous (such as
Tompion) put on their work in order to obtain a better price for
it. There is a story of person bringing to the Tompion workshop
of The Dial and Three Crowns a watch engraved with
Tompion's name as its maker to be repaired. Tompion, recog-
nising the watch as a forgery, smashed it to pieces with a hammer and handed the customer a genuine watch saying, 'Sir,
here is a watch of my making'. One of the functions of the
Clockmakers' Company, formed in 1631, was to stamp out this

129 Long-case clock with the hood removed to show the seat board sitting on the side of the case in an unaltered example.

sort of practice and generally to encourage high standards within in the trade. A fortunate result of this was that most clocks and watches bear their maker's name, making it easier and more enjoyable for collectors to trace the origins and provenance of their old clocks.

The most usual problem area in authenticating a clock is in establishing whether or not the movement and dial are housed in their original case. In the past it was common for some antique dealers to take a handsome case from a 30-hour clock and fit it up with a well-made eight-day movement with a brass dial, probably putting the 30-hour movement and dial into the plainer case. Fortunately now most people know better, but for many clocks it is too late. The movements and dials were not often interchangeable without alteration to the case. While the dial size may have fitted the case aperture perfectly, the board on which the movement sits may have been too high or too low – and in these cases it will seem that the side cheek, on which the seat board sits, may have been cut down or built up. If the alteration has been done recently a new seat board, or one altered with newly-sawn edges or holes for the line, may give it away. Arched-dial clocks and cases are difficult to 'marry' since few arches are of exactly the same portion of a circle and the difference often shows. More glaringly obvious still are examples whose period of making have not been carefully matched or ones which have had strips of wood crudely placed inside the hood door to reduce the aperture for a smaller dial. I saw recently a clock illustrating both these examples of a bad marriage. It was a delightfully small and early eight-day clock with a 10″ square dial by Thomas Cruttenden of York, 1680, cased in a rather large mahogany and oak example from Lancashire or Yorkshire, and made about 1820. Examples such as these should be observed for they form an ideal testing ground for one's knowledge.

If a movement is wrongly cased and a pleasing clock results, then no great harm has been done, for the two parts were anyway made by different craftsmen. I am not suggesting that this is a desirable practice but suggest that the results are preferable to live with than a marriage between a movement and a dial. This latter practice has already been mentioned in the chapter dealing with 30-hour clocks but the practice was by no means restricted to long-case clocks. I have seen all kinds of clocks where this practice, usually badly done, has spoiled a good clock. The signs to look for are spare holes left in the front plate of a movement, where dial feet from a previous dial have been planted. These are rarely filled-in by a clock bodger.

Occasionally bent dial-feet are seen. This is done to get them to clear an obstruction in the motion work of a movement or even to fit them into a crude and inaccurately drilled new hole. It is quite possible to find a clock made not only with components from two clocks, but three or maybe four lots of parts may have been put together to make one saleable clock. But the signs are there if you are able to read them.

One area of faking which is fully recognised by horological scholars, but cheerfully dismissed as nonsense by many present-day owners of these clocks, is the quasi-17th-century water-clock consisting of an oak frame, a crude brass dial with a large counter-balanced hand controlled by a chain and a float, which presumably was intended to descend as water siphoned from one cistern to the other. Examination will often show a cast, not engraved, dial-plate and modern methods of construction of some parts. The top of the float cistern is often rolled over a steel wire to form the edge. An engraved plate, often on the lower cistern or in that area of the clock, proclaims an early origin and a fictitious maker. The example (Plate 130) shown informs us that 'Night Cometh' and that Edward Larkins of Winchester made it in 1621. A more likely explanation is that the clock was made in Birmingham in the early 20th century, when at least one firm of ornamental brassware manufacturers included them in their catalogues.

The shape of the lantern clock has had an enduring appeal and forms the basis of many clocks made today – though these are not fakes, merely borrowing a quaint and nostalgic shape for commercial reasons. Most of them are small and vary from those with French carriage-clock movements to the cheaply-produced battery-driven mantle-shelf perennial at the other end of the scale. During the last few years, however, a number of lantern clocks have come into the country from a Continental source, bearing the name of Thomas Moore of Ipswich, a reputable maker from the early 18th century. These clocks of the correct size and layout are mass-produced and will not bear a detailed examination, but were carefully prepared by some people in this country to attract the unwary. One that I saw had purposely been weathered and the steelwork rusted, giving it a venerable quality that one might have expected of an original; another example of 'buyer beware' for a little knowledge can be a dangerous thing.

It is often said that an old English clock never wears out; within that saying there is a lot of truth, but it needs clarifying. What can be done and what should be done are two different things,

130 Spurious water clock, signed Edward Larkins of Winchester.

and techniques employed must be suitable to avoid expensive damage to a movement or dial. The definition is often quite subtle and based on feeling and experience for old clocks more than on engineering skill. Old English clocks, like any other machines with moving parts, do of course eventually wear, but the way in which the majority are made, with generous use of good materials and incorporating sensible design, means that most parts can be repaired or compensated for wear by a variety of techniques. It is perfectly possible to restore most clocks to full working condition without affecting their value or originality if the restorer has the correct degree of feeling and knowledge. Many jobs that he will have to do will involve undoing the damage done by generations of unskilled bodgers who seemed particularly prevalent in the field of clockwork. This kind of restoring is particularly taxing and will in some cases need skills equal to, if not more than, those required in making a new clock from raw materials. Chapter-rings that have been chrome-plated, escapements that have been savagely mutilated and plates that have been distorted by punch-marks and hammer blows are the sort of damage that I have in mind–and are extremely hard to deal with successfully. If you are fortunate enough to have acquired a clock which is sub-stantially as made, then wear and neglect may have taken a toll of its appearance and functions, making some restoration work necessary on movement dial and case. It is not by any means desirable to keep old clocks in a grubby and worn condition for while this is an undoubted indication of their age it is mis-guided to keep them that way. When made they were pre-sented bright and fresh, their metal parts silvered, polished or gilt, with the cases newly polished to show off the grain or inlays of their wood. When carefully done, restoration can return them to this state in which their makers intended them, and substantially increase their value and visual appeal.

First we shall deal with the wooden case, for this is an impor-tant area in most clocks. Naturally I shall not go into the finer points of cabinet-making, as I have neither the knowledge or the experience, but will concentrate on those areas which can be easily understood and which I hope will make good sense to the clock owner. In long cases stability is all important, and rickety fittings such as the seat board and its union with cheeks at the top of the trunk sides need to be made stable so that they will support the heavy weights and allow the movement a firm enough base to run correctly. If a seat board is thin and seen to bend or has been damaged by splitting or woodworm, then it will need to be replaced with a piece of old oak, which is the most suitable wood. A copy of the old shape will need to be made carefully, for as well as needing two square holes for the gut lines to run from the barrels it will need to be relieved at the back to clear the pendulum rod. It may also be similarly relieved at the front if calendar work or other functions are present in the bottom half of the dial. Small areas could need to be scooped out on the front edge where various pieces project from behind the dial plate. The bottom movement pillars usually accommodate a pair of fasteners which hook over the pillars, and are tightened up by a nut from below, thus making the movement firm with the seat board. This makes handling much easier since the looped ends of the weight pulley-lines have also to be fastened in to the board. If the movement and its supporting board were not firmly connected a tangle could easily ensue.

The seat board may just sit on top of the trunk cheeks but is held in some cases by wood screws, which are usually a later addition. Thirty-hour clocks' seat boards are often a fixture in the case, being nailed to the cheeks with square hand-made nails. Since there is no need to fasten the loop end of the gut line into the seat board on these examples, the board is not usually lifted off with the movement as in eight-day work. In the case of a 30-hour clock the holes in the seat board are quite different since we are only concerned with the descent of a single weight. Although the source of the rope or chain is from two pulleys in the clock, this hangs through a single slot, cut on a shallow curve rather like a dog's hind leg. This allows for the offset of the driving pulleys in the clock and also means that the weight pulley and ropes can be lifted through the slot while allowing the seat board to remain in the case. If seat-board alterations are made it is as well to check, before making the final fixing, that the dial fits nicely up to the aperture in the hood door and fits equally at either side. This is also an important check to make when setting up a clock for often there is sufficient sideways movement to leave an unsightly gap at one side of the dial.

The condition of the mouldings and the state of the glue should also be looked at carefully. The mouldings under the hood form a surface on which the hood slides on to the case. Slots of wood, glued just above these and on the rising checks of the case side boards prevent the hood from toppling forward as it is being slid on and off. Check that they are firmly fixed. One of the most important areas in which the glued joints between mouldings and carcase wood need to be secure is in the region of the waist of the case, at the point where trunk joins base. Very often the thinly-cut moulding and the backboard which may no longer be firm, are all that keep the case upright at this

131 Glue blocks used to strengthen the joint between backboard and side of a long-case clock, circa 1830. These are part of the original construction.

132 Replacement frets for the hoods of long-case clocks. Paper on the surface of the upper one has not yet been sanded away.

point. If there is much looseness here it is as well to take the case to an experienced cabinet-maker, as very often the backboard will have to be strengthened and the inside of the case braced with a number of glue blocks and at the same time the mouldings will need to be refixed in a way which will not spoil the appearance of the wood's old surface. Split panels, missing veneers, and marquetry work will likewise need to be dealt with by an expert. Where an old wooden fret, such as those fitted above the dial in the frieze of the hood, is damaged or missing, a suitable replacement can usually be fretted out by a clockmaker who is capable of making clock hands, for the same kind of skills apply. Since the wood used will need to be little more than a thick veneer, a method has to be devised to stop it splitting along the grain during the fretting operation. Two methods are used to overcome this problem and one of them is to paste paper back and front of the wood to help hold the grain. The other is to cut two frets at once and back these with a strip of thin wood or hardboard during the cutting. The paper on the front piece of wood will need to be a drawing of the design. This is put together to make a sandwich with glue carefully placed only at the edges, so that the final cut when the strips of wood are cut to width, will remove the glued portions and allow the frets to separate. It only remains to sand off the paper on the surface which will be seen. Old frets and some wooden inlays were similarly prepared in manufacture. I have frequently seen such scraps of printed paper when taking old work to pieces.

At the top of the hood, holes which have formed a base for finials are frequently widened or broken away at the edges, particularly if they were mounted on short square plinths or drilled in an applied block behind the centre of a broken arch or swan neck pediment. Glue blocks can easily be replaced and holes can be filled with a piece of shaped soft wood before re-drilling a hole the correct size. If finials were orginally fitted and are now missing, look round for a suitable set as they improve the appearance of a clock enormously. Good reproduction finials are now made in a number of patterns and these do not look out of place if old replacements are unobtainable. There are various views on the polishing of brassware on clock cases. Fortunately there is not very much brass visible, but the average long-case usually has an escutcheon or lock-plate and acorn hinges to the trunk door. The hood may have brass capitals and bases to its columns and brass paterae may decorate the terminals of a swan-necked pediment. In my view these should be bright and clean and once this has been achieved they should be lacquered over. Repeated cleaning of brassware with metal polish tends to fill in the lower portions of the design with a milky deposit of metal polish and polishing also affects the surrounding wood in a similar unfortunate way. To avoid this, care needs to be taken in cleaning the brasswork; however, you may prefer to leave it in a dull unpolished condition whose appearance merges it into the surrounding wood.

One of the most common breakages that can occur in dealing with cases is of the glass in a hood door. A hood removed from the case should always be placed with its face to the wall. Since it is face- or front-heavy it will always fall that way if knocked over and broken glass will be the result. Many clocks will be found to have had the glass replaced, some with the wood of the door badly damaged as a result. Patience is required in removing the old hard putty and an extremely sharp wood chisel is the best tool for this job. This putty is then cut away. On later clocks where a strip of crossbanding or a mahogany veneer is found to form the front of the glass rebate, even more care is required. A hidden danger in this operation is present if you allow the door frame to slide about on the bench while removing the old putty – particles of grit and glass will badly scratch the polished surface. For this reason I keep a grip on the door frame with a wood-carver's vice whose jaws are covered with cork. I then turn the door as each side is carefully cleaned up. Any good glass merchant can cut even the most complicated arched dial shape, but take the door with you so that it is his responsibility to fit the glass. This is one area where measurements are not enough. Putty, normally grey, can easily be coloured by the addition of pigment such as oil paint or powder paints. A middle-brown shade looks good with the wood of most cases.

133 Original reinforcing blocks, shown in the construction of a hood with swan neck pediment.

Old glass can be identified by its imperfections and the lack of uniformity in its thickness. Occasionally it may not be flat and pulls away as much as $\frac{1}{4}$" from the corners of the hood door. If the lenticle glass in the trunk door gets broken, it can be replaced in the same way. A bull's-eye glass is a much more difficult proposition. It would be wrong to use a modern bull's-eye of the type commercially available; an old piece of glass will need to be found. I recently discovered and obtained two of these from a workman's cottage built about 1800 and due for demolition, but this was a very lucky find. Fortunately the thin edges of the glass did not break when the glass cutter was applied, and I was able to make the first one into a suitable oval with no breakage.

A freize of blue glass is often found on the hoods of long-cases from the north-west. This occurs on both square and arched cases and on an arched hood is made in two panels. The glass is usually decorated in patterns of scrolling rococo arabesques, usually accompanied by a centrally placed urn or similar classical feature. The gold-painted pattern is frequently rubbed and needs retouching, which may be quite easily done with a high-quality paint or gold leaf and requires the same skills as those possessed by a dial painter, namely a steady hand and a knowledge of the type of decoration used in old work.

While the basic reason behind cleaning a clock movement is to remove the dirt, old oil and grit to reduce wear on the moving parts, it is gratifying to polish the metal and make a complete and thorough job of the restoration, repairing all broken parts and replacing those which are missing. This way it should be a long time before the plates will need to come apart again. The following paragraphs give some indication of the kind of problems that might be encountered in a movement and what can be done to improve them.

By far the most common ill is wear to the pivot holes in the plates. Any wear that goes uncorrected will allow the wheels and pinions to have the wrong engagement or depth and wear will in turn occur on the pinion leaves and eventually on the teeth of the brass wheels. In correcting this wear, it is essential that the new bushes installed in the plates are not left too tight, as it takes very little friction to stop a clock, particularly in the higher-geared wheels at the top of the train. Perceptible horizontal movement (end shake) must also be retained between the plates and the shoulders of the pinion. The worn pivot holes are enlarged with a five-sided cutting broach or reamer, sufficient to admit a brass bush whose central hole is fractionally tighter than the hole required. The bush is riveted home, filed level with the plate, and polished before the hole is correctly sized to give a snug fit to the pivot. Before this is done the pivot should be examined carefully, for a worn hole is always accompanied by a worn pivot. Most wear will have occurred at the point where the pivot bears on the plate and the end of the pivot which pokes through the plate will not have worn at all. This gives a dumb-bell look to a worn pivot. The pivot will need to be mounted in a lathe and filed up until it is reduced to an overall parallel shape. The pivot is polished and is then ready to be tried in the new bush. It is necessary to fit the arbor between the plates and try it for a free running fit before trying it in relation to the other wheels, when the question of depth of engagement between the wheel and pinion is another factor

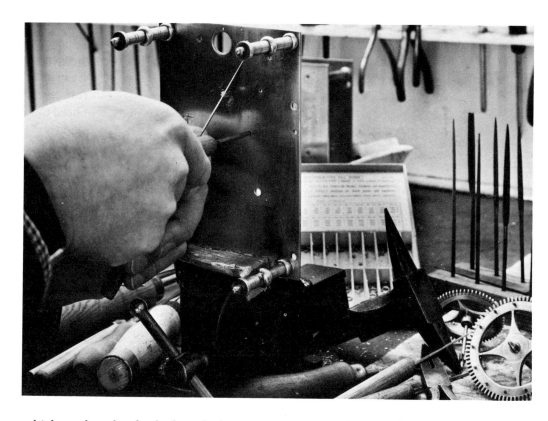

which needs to be checked. Both these tests are necessary before final re-assembly of the movement. It is easy to identify a
tight pivot this way and almost impossible to do it once the
clock has been assembled.

If the clock has been neglected for a long time many bushes
may require attention. I recently restored an eight-day striking
clock which needed twelve in both its trains. Two of the
pinions were worn so thin that they had to be broken off and
replaced. This is not an easy job and in order to do it one needs a
lathe and an accurate chuck, for the area to be drilled is small
and needs to be drilled in the very centre. The depth of the hole
will need to be at least that of the length of the pinion to be
formed. A piece of pinion steel or silver steel will then be
prepared to be a tight fit and driven home.

Escapement faults are also common on worn house-clocks
and are particularly tricky to correct if they have previously
been repaired by an unskilled hand. It is essential that the
pallet arbor does not have worn pivots and it will be necessary
to ensure that there is no up and down movement here if an
anchor escapement is to be correctly impulsed by the escapement teeth, thus retaining its momentum. Ruts worn in the
faces of the pallets will need to be ground or stoned out and the

134 A clock backplate in the
process of rebushing. Cutting
broaches of all sizes may be
seen. The bush to be
inserted in the new hole is
held on the second broach
also in the clockmaker's
hands. The small anvil is
fixed in the vice when
riveting the bushes firm.

pallets re-polished. A file will not touch the extremely hard surfaces that are needed at these points. Once this is done it will be found that the pallets do not have sufficient engagement with the escape wheel and will require closing slightly in order to overcome the excessive drop. This requires great care if breakage is not to occur. The arms of the escapement need to be softened with heat and they can then be closed slightly by squeezing them in a vice. A little distance will be all that is required and, so that one can see what progress has been made, it will be a help if a measurement is taken beforehand with a pair of dividers. The pallets have to be measured outside the vice, for the steel is springy and opening of the vice will mean that the pallets return some way towards their previous gaps. It may be found that unskilled repairers have achieved this repair by lowering the back of the escapement arbor, often by removing the steady pins from the back cock and cutting the screw holes into slots. The pallet arbor can then be roughly dropped into depth, but it will be out of line and out of square with the escape wheel. This type of repair should be corrected as it spoils the appearance of the movement and causes more wear to occur in the escapement. Another common escapement pallet repair is done to save grinding out the ruts caused by the action of the pallets on the escape wheel. This is to cover the faces with a piece of thin steel, such as a portion of pendulum-suspension spring. These are fixed by tinning the pallets with soft solder before applying the cleaned and fluxed pieces of spring. When cool this can be tidied up with a file, and if well done can make a very acceptable repair. Although not as hard as the original face, the repair will withstand many years of wear.

A verge escapement will need its pallet arbor pivots to be in good order. The rear suspension, usually a knife-edge or V-shaped extension to the arbor runs in a brass V-slot and is particularly susceptible to wear. This can, however, easily be built up and refiled to shape. Depth can be adjusted on these escapements by raising or lowering the crown-wheel arbor. Placed vertically in the clock, the bottom pivot revolves on an adjusting screw placed in the underside of the bottom cock. Screwing this in further raises the escape wheel and unscrewing it allows the wheel to drop.

The moon dial is a feature which adds to the value and interest in many old clocks, but frequently they are disconnected or in a bad state of repair. When old clocks were not so well thought-of as they are today these 'unnecessary details' were considered clock-stoppers and many of the connecting links and wheels for calendar- and moon-work were committed to the repairer's scrap box. Dials in the arch of the dial are remote from the hour pipe from which the drive is provided. As a result, repair of this type of moon dial involves the most work. Various methods are used to give the disc its impetus, moving it on one tooth every twelve hours; it is often difficult to see which method was used if all the old work has been removed. Most moon discs have escapement or saw-like inclined teeth; this indicates that they are advanced by a pin or a peg revolving on a twelve-hour wheel or pushed by a slotted or jointed lever pivoted on to the back of the dial. Very rarely, however, the teeth are conventional wheel-teeth and are in constant mesh with the motion wheels, driven by the hour wheel. Whatever method was used it can be tricky to reproduce, but a good restorer should be able to take this sort of work in his stride. If wheels are missing for moon- or calendar-work, they can easily be cut after working out the number of teeth required and the pitch of gearing needed to work with the existing wheels. Date-work of the open lunette type with a fan-shaped portion of the date disc visible through this aperture is only rarely removed. Such an action spoils the appearance of the clock by leaving a large hole in the dial. It was far easier simply to remove the pin which pushed on the teeth. Calendar indications by a hand needs two wheels behind the dial to make them work; they are often found to have one of their intermediary wheels, the 24-hour wheel, removed. The wheel immediately behind the dial will generally be in place, for the calendar hand is screwed into it, and each holds the other in place. The most usual type of calendar is the box type, with a large internally toothed ring running behind the dial's surface and showing the date through a box in the lower part of the dial plate. This also needs a 24-hour wheel and pin to advance it. This 24-hour wheel is very often missing and replacing this is a regular task in a restorer's workshop.

A leaf broken from a steel pinion almost certainly means that a replacement has to be made for this is impossible to repair. Teeth are frequently found to be broken from a brass wheel. This is a problem which occurs when the mainspring of a clock breaks or comes adrift from its anchorage in the spring barrel. The shock imposed on the train often does much damage, especially to pivots, wheels and pinions. If the number of teeth broken is not too great – perhaps up to three – repair is feasible. More than this and it is usually easier to replace the whole wheel. To replace teeth, the wheel rim is cut with a wedge-shaped gap of the required length; a piece of brass scrap of the same thickness as the wheel is shaped into a tightly-fitting

135 Side view of a 30-hour movement and dial. The toothed discs behind the dial, both advanced by the same pin, can be clearly seen. The top one moves a halfpenny moon and the bottom a lunette calendar.

136 A clockmaker's bench showing various tools and movement parts. At the left can be seen a piercing saw used for cutting out clock hands, brass frets and so on. The small open box in the centre contains a variety of fine punches. The hand tools in the foreground are reamers and cutting broaches. In the background centre, standing in a block, can be seen a selection of needle files.

wedge of the same size as the gap and let in with soft solder. The teeth can be fretted and filed up with a piercing saw and needle files. Care and a steady hand will usually give first-class results. After polishing a good repair should be barely perceptible. Often wheel-teeth have been pushed over by a sudden force such as that caused by a breaking spring. Straightening them is not often successful as they tend to be brittle. This should only be done by leverage applied from the root at the next good tooth, otherwise further damage may result. The teeth will usually break off as they are straightened or be weakened enough to crumble later. It is usually best to replace them right away.

Faults in strike work are extremely common and wear in these parts will usually result in the strike being run together and unable to stop after striking the appropriate number, or not being able to strike at all. Most faults are as a result of breakage or wear, and often an unskilled repair means that the work has to be done again. In rack-striking examples the small pallet which gathers up the rack during striking may have dropped off its square, causing continual striking until the weight is removed. The rack-tail is often found to be badly bent or in-expertly soldered together. Both these parts can be easily remade. Wear in lifting-pieces, hammer-tails, locking-pieces and count-wheels can all be overcome, but experience is necessary otherwise the correct sequence of strike action will not be understood. Repairs of this type are therefore best left to an expert restorer.

Eight-day clock-lines and thirty-hour clock ropes are still relatively cheap and should be replaced each time the clock is cleaned, or sooner if they show signs of wear. This point applies even more to clocks with a greater duration than eight days for a clock going a longer period will have heavier weights. A broken line will result in a falling weight and possibly damage to the base of the case or even floor-boards. Gut is the traditional material for clock lines, made from the twisted lining of a sheep's stomach. It is perfectly adequate for most weight clocks and looks correct on old clocks. However, for a clock with very heavy weights, it may be safer to consider a modern brass wire line coated with plastic. These lines are soft and pliable in use, will not damage the clock and will last longer than gut lines. They can also be used with considerable success in connecting a spring barrel and fusée, in bracket and English-dial-clock restoration.

Whether or not a 30-hour pull-wind clock is equipped with rope or chain to support the weight, problems are bound to occur. To find out which was original to the clock, the spiked pulleys inside the movement will need to be examined. A rope pulley has an even surface in its valley, interrupted only by five or six spikes arranged to stop the rope slipping as it drives the trains. A pulley intended for use with a chain will have cut-away sections or depressions between the spikes, intended to accommodate the obverse link of the chain. The chain will need to be of a measured pitch in order to lie smoothly over the pins as the pulley revolves. A chain of incorrect pitch will jump, causing possible damage and irritating and unexpected noise. It is possible to run a chain clock with a rope but not the other way round as the obverse link would stop the other from settling firmly over the spikes, even if these were of the correct pitch.

Specially-made ropes are available from material dealers. These have a loose weave in order to give grip on the pulley spikes. I managed to have some good hemp rope made up by a specialist rope-maker. This works out rather expensive but makes a long-lasting job, and does not shred as much as the more usual cotton rope. Worn spikes or an unsuitable 'hard' rope will allow the rope to slip, usually during the strike and particularly when fully wound. This greatly reduces the duration of 30-hours (which is all too short anyway) and may in extreme cases cause the weight to drop to the floor in one massive slide. Spikes are replaceable by taking the pulley to pieces and screwing or pulling out the worn ones. New ones can be made from silver steel and put back before riveting the pulley back together. The disc type of click-spring for the pull-wind may be checked at the same time. These are often worn and loose on their rivets. At this stage this spring can be re-riveted or remade depending on its state of repair. In fitting a new rope a decision needs to be made about the way in which the ends are joined together. This needs to slide over pulleys and cause no obstruction. I find it best to butt-joint the rope after first binding round the two separate ends. The two are placed end to end and sewn together by stitches coming from behind and among the binding. This in turn is wrapped round and stitched through carefully. This is done with a fine but strong bookbinder's thread, which I have found to be excellent and lasts for years. When correctly spiked and equipped with a new rope the problems of dust and fluff in the movement caused by the rope passing through the pulleys remain. It is a problem we can do little about. The movement will need to be dismantled and cleaned more regularly than others.

Pendulums are fragile and very easily broken. It is fortunate therefore that they are also easily repaired. At the top the suspension spring will snap suddenly if knocked or bent too far. It is easy to do this while transporting a clock and while fitting the pendulum into the clock case. New springs are readily available from the material dealers and come complete with the top brass by which the pendulum will hang from the movement back cock. The suspension is held into the brass block by a single rivet which is easily punched out and later replaced. If the block is worn or, as is often the case, mis-shapen because of repeated spring replacements this too should be replaced. A replacement can easily be filed up in the workshop, or it is possible to buy a suspension with top brass and brass block complete and ready to screw on to the pendulum rod. Adjustment will have to be made in individual cases but this usually only involves filing a little off the thickness of the block to achieve a sliding fit in the escapement crutch—essential to good running of the clock—or reducing the length of the suspension spring which naturally needs to vary from clock to clock. This is done by punching out the lower rivet and shearing a portion from the suspension spring before returning it to the slot and tapping back in the securing rivet. A smooth finish is essential on the flanks of the block and its point of contact with the crutch should be as near the centre of the block's length as possible. A badly damaged or roughly repaired pendulum rod can easily be replaced with a length of $\frac{1}{8}''$ wire. A 4BA thread at the top and bottom of the rod will usually secure it into the block and the tapered iron blade at the bottom on which the bob slides. If the hole is too large at this point then the rod may be silver-soldered neatly into position. It is essential to check that the pendulum bob is a free sliding fit up and down over this blade, as easy adjustment of timekeeping depends on it. A pendulum which has fallen or been dropped may have broken or damaged the rating thread and nut at the very bottom of the pendulum. It is not unknown for this portion to spear the floorboards when suspension breakage unexpectedly occurs. The rating nut and its threaded stud are also easily replaced. The pendulum should be arranged by the length of its rod, to have good adjustment both up and down, when the clock is keeping good time. This way the clock may be brought to time with ease, should a change in the rate occur. Most people find that house clocks with a long pendulum need attention twice a year. When the weather cools in the autumn, clocks tend to gain and the pendulum will need lengthening, and with the return of milder weather in the spring the pendulum will need to be marginally shorter.

The last job in setting up a movement in the workshop is to oil its pivots, levers and other parts which move against each other. However, the wheels and pinions should never be oiled as brass and steel will work together quite easily in a dry state. To coat them with oil would simply encourage the adhesion of dust and dirt and cause increased wear in the pinions. A special clock oil made with qualities suited to a slow moving mechanism should be used. A good clock oil will stay where it is placed and not run down the plates or move along the arbors and on to the pinions. It will also stay liquid and remain in a non-sticky state for a long time. If a clock has been thoroughly cleaned and degreased during restoration, the initial oiling will probably last only a few months, particularly if the clock is housed in a warm dry centrally-heated atmosphere. Afterwards annual oiling should be quite sufficient. Since the oil needs to be carefully placed, a precise method of doing so involves using a clock oiler. This need be no more than length of 20-gauge wire bent at one end into a loop holder and at the other flattened by a hammer blow into a spade which will pick up a drop of oil from the bottle. This can then be accurately placed where it is needed in the movement.

There are many occasions when attention to clock hands is

necessary. Very often old repairs have been carried out by plating from behind. This makes a strong but unsightly job. The plating and soft solder has to be warmed and cleaned off before a more delicate repair is carried out with silver solder, butt-jointing the parts and afterwards removing all excess solder with needle files. Steel hands can then be blued by heat in the traditional manner. Only a small yellowish line of solder will then be seen and this is easily touched over with a spot of matt black paint before oiling the surface of the warm hand. When repaired carefully with silver solder brass hands can be polished so that the repair is almost impossible to detect. The hands should be protected with a transparent lacquer before returning to the clock. Hand collets are often overlooked in restoration. These too should be brightly polished and fastened with a neatly fitting pin, to give the perfect finish to a handsome pair of hands.

There are no hard and fast rules for the making up of a woman's face. Dial restoration needs to be approached in the same manner, bearing in mind that each will require a different degree of attention. Brass dials tend to lose their gleam over the years, and when breaks in the lacquered finish occur they allow the surface underneath to deteriorate fairly quickly. These can be caused by a careless scratch with the winding key or by a finger while pushing on the hands. The silver deposit on chapter rings blackens and the brass dial plate will turn dirty with green markings that will eventually eat into the plate, causing pitting and deterioration of the surface. For this reason alone it is essential that a brass dial is kept in good clean order and lacquered against the corrosive tendencies of the atmosphere. As a rule chapter rings, calendar and seconds circle were silvered to contrast with the gilt or polished brass of the dial plate corners and its matted centre. On later brass-dialled clocks, particularly those produced in the north, an engraved centre may also have been filled with black wax and silvered. Spandrel casting and dial plates may still exhibit signs of their original gilt surface. Since it is almost impossible to have this restored today, preservation of this surface is essential. First of all it should be washed in domestic washing-up liquid and very hot water, perhaps aided by a nail brush to remove the dirt. If this is not successful in restoring the surface, a very weak solution of ammonia should be tried, which should be washed off almost immediately and the part washed in clean warm water afterwards. It will be impossible to achieve the brilliance of a newly gilt surface, but a surface which looks clean and retains a good measure of the warm glow associated with a gilded surface could be considered a success. Silvered surfaces may be restored but the secret lies in preparation of the parts. These are usually rings which require rubbing-down with a circular motion to obtain a good matt brass surface, free from scratching, grease or any other imperfections which will spoil the surface. The wax-filled engraving will usually be intact and rubbing-down of the plate surface will not affect this. After silvering the wax will be unaffected and continue to show as a good black. I rub down with a variety of materials but usually finish with a fine pumice powder worked with a cloth pad. Some restorers use an electric wheel, rather like a potter' wheel. This spins the rings, which are finished by holding an emery cloth against them; this gives a uniform and mechanical appearance to the chapter-ring, rather like the surface of a gramophone record. This is not generally considered to be good practice as it is too mechanical and uniform a way to restore an antique finish. It may also be harmful to the engraved surface if done too vigorously. The silver surface is imparted to the brass by the chemical action of silver chloride paste and tartaric acid. This is applied evenly on a piece of cotton wool and rubbed into the surface. The ring is then polished, or at least rubbed to a good white, by the application of a creamy paste of tartaric acid in water. The ring needs to be dried quickly by dabbing with a clean linen or cotton cloth and then left in a dry atmosphere for a while before lacquering. Like the solid metal, silvering will rapidly tarnish if unprotected. The old craftsmen used a lacquer made by dissolving shellac in alcohol but a more expedient and lasting method is available today. A transparent cellulose lacquer may be brushed on. Care will have to be taken in the application, however, for the lacquer may tend to melt the engraver's wax and if these areas are lingered upon or the brush is rubbed over them several times then the black may be picked up and spoil the silvering. The same lacquer will usually be suitable for finishing all surfaces on the dial, including the polished brass and the cast spandrel decorations.

There is no short-cut to the skills required in restoration of a painted dial. One is either capable of the brushwork and lettering needed or not. If not then the work should be entrusted to an expert restorer. Many dials have been badly re-painted and the beauty of the original lost. Removal of the unskilled paint job is sometimes possible and then often the signs 'photographed on the dial plate' enable a good dial restorer to put back the original character of the dial's black work. As stated earlier the polychrome sections were usually painted in oil-bound colours and are generally well preserved. Exceptions to

137 A newly-silvered chapter ring giving a good black-and-white effect, on a lantern clock by Richard Fennel of Kensington.

187

this come in various ways. A dial whose surface has been chipped or burnt (with a candle) is occasionally seen; these have to be patched. Colour-work on a brass ground such as found in a moon disc or rocking-figure backing sheet does not hold quite so well as it does on iron, and frequently needs touching up around its edges. A dial which has suffered a blow or a fall will have sections where the paint and background has come away from the metal. Dial feet which have worked loose will also have caused the ground to chip and crumble. Most of these repairs can be dealt with successfully by filling and matching the colours. Artist's oil colours should be used mixing with a quick-drying medium such as Winton retouching varnish for the pictorial work. Care must be taken to use the colours in the same way as the original and not put thick blobs of paint where the original was built up in thin delicate layers. Mixing the correct colour for the dial ground is often the trickiest job of all, and most will be found to be a delicate green or brown tint and not white as we might suppose. Most dials are restorable with the right amount of expertise except perhaps those on which a good part of the ground has perished or started to lift away from the metal. The hard fine surface achieved by the old dial-making firms is difficult if not impossible to copy. It was probably done by a stoving type of process and to do this on large sections of the dial while attempting to preserve the original section is a tall order. Once the dial's surface has been restored, cleaned and degreased the painting of the chapters, moon indication's name and so on, in black can take place. The various concentric circles – and there are often quite a few – can best be put on with a ruling pen and black ink, the lettering and numberwork with a variety of fine brushes and signwriter's black paint. Any retouching of the coloured areas should come next as it is essential for the black line to be done first when the surface is free of grease, enabling the ink to flow freely from the pen. After the artwork is complete it will need to dry in a warm atmosphere for a few days before the dial is given a final surface. What should be done next is a matter of some debate, but to cover all the surface with a shiny varnish is definitely wrong, and although giving a lasting finish will look wrong and destroy the correct period look that is necessary in such a dial. In the old workshops, only the colour work was varnished.over and the black work left unprotected. This accounts for the eventual loss by washing of so many dial features and names. An improvement on this method is one I use, which goes a long way towards preserving an authentic appearance and also adds a little to the preservation factor. Colour-work is varnished over in panels using a light thin artist's varnish such as Winton picture varnish. This is quick-drying and colourless. Once this is dry the rest is given a coat of wax polish. When polished up with a soft clean cloth this gives a good protective finish and a sheen which is very acceptable.

By virtue of their tall thin shape long-case clocks are precarious and require very careful placing, if stability and safety are to be achieved. Stability is of course essential if the clock is to run properly and if the safety of the clock is ignored it may mean total destruction. I was once called upon to restore what was left of a clock after it had fallen on its face and then down a flight of stairs. Setting up the clock should start with the choice of position. This should be away from a busy or precarious part of the house. A quiet corner of the hall or landing has traditionally been a favourite place, although I do not actually advise that a case should be placed across a corner: an additional wooden support will be needed to make the clock adequately secure and stable. It is not necessary to go to the length of securing a case to a flat wall with screws. The many holes in the backboards of old clock cases indicate to us how common this practice was in the past. The following procedure will give excellent results and make the clock secure by use of its own weight. First of all obtain a piece of wood slightly less wide than the case but equal in thickness to any skirting board that may be in the room. Fix this wood to the outside of the backboard at about the height of the top of the hood door. Two $1\frac{1}{4}''$ panel pins are usually enough to stop this piece of wood falling. Place the case back in contact with the wall an cut two more small pieces of wood each about $\frac{3}{4}''$ thick. These should then be placed under the two front corners of the case at a point where base moulding or feet reaches the floor. The case should now stand level from all angles, and because the front corners are lifted clear of the floor, all weight of movement, weights and so on, will cause the clock to be pushed firmly against the wall, and be held securely. An uneven floor should be compensated for in a block placed under the front feet to make the case vertical. Appearances are all-important here and it is unnecessary actually to check a clock's setting with a spirit level at any stage. Next the seat board and movement should be lifted into place and held secure until the weights are hung on the pulleys ensuring that it cannot fall forwards. While doing this, check that the lines are gathered on to the winding barrels and have not slipped round arbors or into the ratchet click and spring wheel which make winding possible. The movement should now run on vigorously until the pendulum is lifted into the case, slipped upwards through the crutch and hung on its supporting cock. The final part of the setting-up now needs to be done. This is an adjustment common to most clocks using a pendulum and is not restricted to the long-case variety alone. First however, temporarily place the hood on to the case and check that the movement is centrally placed; if too far back or to one side, it will leave an unsightly gap between case and dial. Adjust this before finally setting-up the escapement. Remove the hood and set the clock in motion by giving the pendulum a gentle swing. The clock should tick and then tock when the pendulum is equally positioned either side of its centre (or the position at which it will hang when the clock is stopped). If this is taking place to one side the clock will 'limp'. It is then said to be 'out of beat' and the clock will stop after a short while. This problem can be seen by looking into the case when the pendulum is working. Some people prefer to make the adjustment while listening to the beat of the escapement. To adjust, you will have to place both hands behind the movement and feel for the escapement crutch through which the pendulum slides. An escapement action which is exaggerated to the left-hand side of the pendulum swing will mean that a small bend to the right will be needed in the crutch, and vice-versa. The crutch arm is made of bendable iron wire for this purpose. Bending should take place, pushing gently with the thumb of one hand against the wire arm while the other thumb is placed at the top of the wire near its junction with the pallet arbor and take the strain in order that no damage to the escapement occurs. One or two little bends may be necessary but it will be seen that the clock will readily come to beat this way. When done, let the clock settle down and you will soon hear if you have been fully successful. Move the hands to time, allowing the strike to sound out if you are dealing with a count-wheel clock, and similarly the twelve must be allowed to gather in a clock with rack-striking. Check that the moon is correctly phased, and that the date is correctly shown. Finally replace the hood or close the case, check that any finals on the hood are correctly stood to attention. Then put the winding key in a safe place. If everything is carefully done, you may now sit down and admire your handiwork, knowing that the clock will run for many years.

Index

*Figures in italics refer to captions to
the illustrations.*

Accuracy 108, 109, 113, 114, 123
Act of Parliament clock *see* Tavern
  clock
Alarm mechanisms *39*, 92, 95, 96, *97*,
  103, *121*
American clocks 144, 145, *145*, 151
Anchor escapement 14, 30, *89*, 96,
  98, 105, 107, 112, 125, *128*
Apprenticeship 35
Arbor 14, 23, 28
Arched dial clock 42, 59, 75, *82*, *83*
Arch-topped hood *76*, 77
Architectural-topped case 77, *81*, *105*
Austrian clocks 146, 147

Balance-wheel escapement 14, 15, 38,
  90-91, 98
Ball moon 19, *26*, *60*, *158*
Balloon-shaped case *82*, 84, *85*
Barrel 14, 15
Basket-topped clock *81*, *82*, 83
Bedpost clock 89
'Bell metal' 32
Bells 32, 37, 98, *98*, 109, 110, 120
Bell staff 15, 28, 98
Bell-topped case *53*, *82*, *83*, *83*
Bird-and-flower marquetry *61*, 66
Birdcage construction 15, 29, 30, *110*,
  115, 116
Black Forest clock *141*, 145, *145*, 146,
  151
Blade spring 15
Bob pendulum 15
Booth of Pontefract 49, *51*
Boss 15
Bothamley, William 61, *61*, 78
Bowyer, William 91, 99
Bracket clock 8, *33*, 42, 43, 50, 53,
  54, 58, *70*, 71, 81, *81*, 83, *83*, 85,
  85, 123-133, *155*
Brass 23, 24, 28, 44, 58, *112*, 114,
  121, 175, 176
Brass-dial clock 44, 77
Brick-work base *64*, 81
Bridge 15
Broken-arch topped hood *76*, 77, 78,
  78
Buying a clock 168-172

Calendar 40, *52*, *177*, 180
Cartel clock *131*, 140, 143
Cases *61*, 63-85, *100*, 103, 104, 134-
  135, *130*, *131*, *136*, 137, 140, 143,
  144, 147, 173-175
Centre seconds 15
Chamber clock 15, 27, 29, 30, 86, 89
Chapter ring 15, 38, 39, *39*, 40, *41*,
  43, 46, *47*, *177*, 186
Church clock 37, 136
Clements, William 105, 106, *107*
Click 15
Cock 15, 16, 28
Collet 16, 30
Compensated pendulum *112*
Contrate wheel 16
Coster, Salomon 92, 93

Country clocks 31, *33*, 42, 45, *47*, *69*,
  71, *72*, 75, *75*, 79, 112, *112*, 115,
  116, 117, 119
Count-wheel striking 16, *110*, 111,
  112, 115, 118, 125
Creed, Thomas *88*, 92
Cromwellian clocks 90
Crown wheel 16
Crutch 16
Cruttenden, Thomas 100, 171
Cushion-topped clock 75, *75*, *81*

Dating a clock 16, *43*, 97, 115, 140,
  171, 172
Day-of-the-month indicator 16
Deacon, Samuel 118, *165*, 166-167
Dead-beat escapement 16, 113, 114
Detent 17
Dial foot 17
Dial plate 17, *24*, 45, *51*, *124*
Dials 37-62, *81*, *82*, *108*, 135, 136,
  136, 149, *165*, 185-189
Dolphin fret 99, *99*
Drop dial *136*, 139, *139*, 140
Dummy winding squares 117, 118
Dutton, William 78, 115

East Anglian lantern clock *39*,101
Ebony *61*, 63, 66, 67, 83, 84, *124*
Ellicot, John 50, 115
Enamel 50, *53*
Equation-clocks 108, 109
Escapement 17

Fakes 169-172
False plate 17, 49, 53, *63*, *139*, 140
Farrer, John 11, *24*
Feet 64, 75, 84, 98
Finial 17
Flamsteed, John 106
Fly 17, 110
Foliate fret 99, *99*
Foliot balance 15, 17
Fortnum and Mason's clock 37
French clocks *148*, 151
French feet 75
Fret 17, *83*, 98, 99, *99*, *175*
Fromanteel, Ahasuerus 59, 66, 91, 93,
  100, 104, *105*, 152-153, 164
Fusée 17, 123, *126*

Galileo 8, 92
Gamble, Henry 77, *78*
German clocks 145, 146, 151
Gillows of Lancaster 72, *72*, 74, *74*,
  77, 81, 84, *85*, 128
Glass 75, 77, 176, 177
Gongs 18
Gothic style 144, *145*, *148*
Graham, George 113, 155
Grasshopper escapement 155
Grid-iron pendulum 114, 155

Halifax moon 164, *164*
Hands 37-62, 116, *135*, *137*, *139*, 140,
  184, 185

Harrison, John 113, 114, 154-156,
  155
Heraldic fret 99, *99*
Hindley, Henry *41*, *108*, 109, 157-
  158, *158*
Hood 18, 64, 66, 68, 75-79, 134, 175,
  176, *176*
Horned pediment *see* Swan necked
  pediment
Huntsman, Benjamin 25
Huygens, Christiaan 92, 93

Iron 28, 32, 38, *112*, 113, 114, *121*
Iron turret clock 28
Ismay, John *47*, *110*, 116

Jacks 37
Japan work 135
Johnson, Christopher 117
Jones, Henry *124*, *126*, 127

Knibb, Joseph 95, 107, 108

Lacquer 70, 71, 79, *82*, 186
Lantern clock *24*, 27, 28, 30, 38, 39,
  39, 42, *43*, 54, 86-103, *107*, 111,
  118, 177
Larkins, Edward 172, *172*
Latch 18
Latten clock *see* Lantern clock
Leaf 18
Lenticle 18, 66, 67
Levelling a clock 189
Lifting-piece 18, 28, 112
Lion's-mask side handles *82*, *83*, 85
Lister, Thomas 59, *70*, 109
Liverpool base *see* Brickwork base
Long-case clock 8, 9, *10*, 11, *33*, 34,
  41, *51*, *69*, *70*, 74, 79, 104-112,
  121, *126*, *158*, *171*, 189-190
Loomes, Thomas 91, 153
Lowry, Morgan 59, *70*, *109*
Lunette 18

Mahogany 64, 72, 74, *74*, 75, *75*, 76,
  77-81, *81*, 83, 84, 85, 140, 144
Maintaining power 18
Maintenance 95, 173-190
Mantel clock 85, *87*
Marine chronometer 113, 114, 154-
  156, *155*
Marquetry *33*, *51*, *61*, *64*, 67, 68, 71,
  79, 80, 83, 84, *158*
Mean time 108
Modernisation 42, 43, 97, 116, 117
Month clock *51*, 66, 107, 114
Moon dial 19, 25, *26*, *60*, *60*, 61, 164,
  166, *177*, 179, 180
Moore, Thomas 135, 172
Motion work 19
Movement 19, 22, 23
Mudge, Thomas 78, 115
Music barrel 19
Musical clocks 62, *70*, 120, *126*, 161,
  163
Mysterieuse clock *148*, 151

Norris, Edward 24, *26, 89*
Numerals 38, 40, *102*

Oak 63, *64*, 71, 72, *72*, 77, 79, 103, 135, 140
Ogden, Thomas 25, *26*, 57, 60, 77, 117, *158*, 164-166, *165*
Oiling a clock 184
Oliver, Charles 80, *81*
Oriental style 71, 79, *82*, 135, 143
Oyster shell parquetry 68

Pagoda-style hood 71, *76*, 78, *79*
Paint 188, 189
Painted dial 50, *51*, *53*, 186, 188 *see also* White dial
Pallets 19
Parquetry *61*, 67, 82
Pendulum 106-107 *see also* Bob-pendulum, Seconds pendulum
Pillars 19, 28, 79, 80, 81, 105, *107*
Pine 71, 72, 75, 84, 103, 135, 144
Pineapple finials *82*, 85
Pinion 19, 23, 24, *26*, 27, 28
Pivot 20
Plate frame movement 105, *107*, *110*
Plates 20, 23, 28, *128*
Posted frame movement *see* Birdcage construction
Precision regulator 112, 114, 115
Pyke, George *62*, *143*, 158, 161, *163*

Rack-striking 20, *110*, 112, *112*, 118, 125, *126*
Rating nut 20
Recoil 20
Regency style *82*, 83, *83*, 85
Repairing a clock 173-190
Repeat striking facility 20, 111, 112, *124*, 125, 126, *126*
Rocking figures 61, 62, *62*
Rococo style 44, *45*, *127*, 143

Rogers, Isaac 101, 102, *102*
Roman-striking 108
Ropes *93*, 182, 183
Royal pendulum 107

Salisbury Cathedral clock 37
Scafe, William *135*, 137, *138*
Schwanfelder 50, *51*, *53*
Scottish cases *64*, *76*, 79
Screws *24*, 25, 28, 98, 119, 120
Seat board 20
Seaweed marquetry *64*, 67
Seconds hand 40, 57, 58, 107, *135*, *138*
Seconds pendulum 14, 20, 30, 107
Selwood, William *39*, 91, 98, 99, 153
Setting a clock 104, 108, 184, 190
Sheep's head clock 42, 101
Shelf clock 144, 145, *145*
Side glasses 83, *83*
Silvering 21, *177*
Skeleton clock *148*, 148-151
Snail 21
Snow, William 117, *118*, *163*, 167
Solar dial 60
Solar time 108
Spandrel 21, 40-44, 46, 48
Spring-driven clocks 86, *97*, 123
Spurgin, Jeremy *39*, *72*, *89*
Star wheel *126*, 164
Steel 18, 23-25, 28, 58, 123
Stewart, James 128, *128*, *130*
Strike/silent indicator 42, 59
Striking mechanism *see* Count-wheel striking *and* Rack-striking
Swan-necked pediment 75, *76*, 77, 78, *176*

Tavern clock 134-139
Teeth *26*, 27, *132*, 180, 181
Throw 21
Tipling, William *51*, 53, 156-157

Tompion, Thomas 29, 35, *35*, 68, 95, 106, 113, *124*, 126, 153-154, *155*, 170
Tower clock *107*, 136
Towneley, Richard 106, 107
Train 21

Vallin, Nicholas 86
Verge escapement 15, 21, 86, *88*, 94, 95, 97, 98, 101, 111, 123, 124, *124*
Victorian marble clock *82*, 85, *87*
Vienna regulator 146, 147, *147*

Wall clocks 102, *131*, 134-143, *160*
Walnut *64*, 66, *66*, 67, 68, 69, 70, 71, 72, 78, 83
Watches 154, 155, 156
Water clock 172, *172*
Webster, Henry *43*, 96, 98, *98*
Wedges *26*, 28, 29
Weights 21, 31, 32, 91, *93*, *109*, 118, 122, 139
Wetherfield collection 9
Whale's tail cresting *76*, 78
Wheel 21, 26, 27, 28
White-dial 21, *26*, 47-50, 57, *64*, 75, *76*, 79, 115, *121*
Williamson, John *41*, *106*, 156-157, *158*
Wilson, Thomas 79, 80, *81*
Winding *93*, 104, 105, *107*, 109, *109*
Winding holes 40, *41*, 109
Winding squares 21
Winged lantern clock 96
Wood *61*, 63-85, *64*, *66*, *130*, *131*, 173-176
Woolley, James 75, *126*, 162-164
Woolley, John 164

Year clock *34*, 107, *107*, *109*

Acknowledgements

The following kindly allowed their clocks to be illustrated and gave invaluable help in the preparation of the book:
Mrs M. W. Arnold, Mr K. Aspinall, Mrs Christine E. Barker, Mr Granville Barrett, Mr Nelson Bestwick, Miss Rani Butt, Mr David Bavingdon, Mr Donald Cawbourne, Mrs Lynne Finnegan, Mr Dan Finney, Mr Robert Foster, Mr Christopher Gilbert, Mrs Claire Greaves, Mr Frederick Hodgson, Miss M. Lawson, Leeds City Museum, Mr Brian Loomes, C. Lumb and Sons, Ltd., Mrs Janice Lumb, Museum of Lincolnshire Life, Lincoln, Mr Ray M. S. Precious, Mr Paul Rodgers, Mr Wilfred Scatchard, Mr Norman Whitfield, Yorkshire Archaeological Society.

The photographs of items in Abbey House Museum, Kirkstall and Temple Newsam House are reproduced by courtesy of Leeds City Art Gallery, those in Towneley Hall Art Gallery and Museum by courtesy of Burnley Borough Council, illustrations number 3, 62 and 103 by courtesy of the City of Bradford Metropolitan Council Museums Department, Bolling Hall Museum, number 46 by courtesy of Spalding Gentlemen's Society, number 57,

58 and 59 by courtesy of the Archives Department, Westminster City Library.

All the photographs in this book were taken for The Hamlyn Group by David Griffiths with the exception of those listed below:
James Arnfield, Stockport 2, 6, 7, 8, 9, 10, 12; David Barker, Keighley frontispiece, 13, 15, 22, 23, 24, 27, 28, 29, 30, 31, 32, 35, 40, 45, 47, 49, 63, 64, 68, 69, 75, 80, 83, 89, 92, 93, 96, 102, 104, 106, 118, 123, 124, 135; British Museum, London 20, 21, 79, 121; Christie Manson and Woods, London 91; Hamlyn Group Picture Library 87, 110, 111, 113, 114, 116; Hamlyn Group–East Midlands Photographic Services 46; Hamlyn Group–John Webb 57, 58, 65; National Maritime Museum, London 117; Royal Commission on Historical Monuments (England) 16.

The line drawings were made by Samuel McMurran with the exception of those on pages 94, 121 and 133 which were made by David Barker and those on pages 14 and 16 which were made by Bob Mathias.